Abortion and Informed Common Sense

ABORTION AND
Informed
COMMON SENSE

MAX J. SKIDMORE

Westphalia Press
An Imprint of the Policy Studies Organization
Washington, DC
2022

Westphalia Press
An imprint of Policy Studies Organization
1367 Connecticut Avenue NW
Washington, D.C. 20036
info@ipsonet.org

ISBN: 978-1-63723-911-7

Cover and interior design by Jeffrey Barnes
jbarnesbook.design

Daniel Gutierrez-Sandoval, Executive Director
PSO and Westphalia Press

Updated material and comments on this edition
can be found at the Westphalia Press website:
www.westphaliapress.org

To the women of America

and Everywhere Else

TABLE OF CONTENTS

INTRODUCTION

This book grew from a happenstance. Throughout a long life, I have been concerned with human rights. After much thought and study, I have maintained a conviction that abortion is one of those rights, and fits well into the traditional American array of individual freedoms.

The controversy over a woman's "right to choose," as opposed to the numerous "rights" that abortion opponents decide should be assumed to exist for "unborn children," has always struck me as incomplete. Two missing elements of the argument seems obvious, yet they remain almost completely overlooked.

The first is that there is virtually no consideration whatever of the pregnant person, herself. Her rights, if she even is assumed to have any at all, do not in any way enter into consideration, unless possibly if the pregnancy appears to threaten her life (to be sure, some more humane anti-abortionists do concede, often grudgingly, that no one should have to carry to term a pregnancy caused by rape, but the point remains).

Second, and most paradoxically, opponents of abortion appear also generally to be opposed to "big government," yet all the while they refuse to recognize any rights at all that belong to the person who is pregnant, and to be comfortable with complete control over her. The opponents seem oblivious to the clear fact that stripping pregnant adults of all ability to determine their future requires enormously powerful, virtually totalitarian, government.

There is even confusion about what it is that constitutes "big government." No one should underestimate the irrationality of contemporary politics. Many citizens easily swallow the camel of complete prohibition of abortion, Patriot Acts, Wars on Drugs, harsh prison sentences for improper voting (even when motivated by misunderstanding), and the like.

In the guise of "freedom," though, the same citizens often choke on gnats. Minor infringements on comfort designed to protect health cause threats of revolution. Requiring vaccination for Covid to participate in various public activities becomes proof that "government" is seeking to regiment the population. Wearing masks in public is a sign of vanished "liberty," while urging the practice of social distancing becomes totalitarianism. Years of anti-government propaganda that now has completely subsumed the Republican Party have caused huge resentment of procedures intended to safeguard health, rather than resentment of the virus that causes a worldwide pandemic.

Resentment should be directed toward austerity, toward traditional desires to keep government as small as possible. This has prevented measures that should have been in place years ago to protect against pandemics that experts have warned would be inevitable. Warnings came not only from medical experts. I warned years ago that such measures would be essential.[1]

Many circumstances today make it clear that women suffer under misogynistic practices. There are draconian state laws, continued Republican packing of the Supreme Court with ideologues, hearings before that Court regarding an extreme anti-abortion law from Mississippi, and an especially unusual and invasive new law from Texas. If all that and more were not enough to convince me, a concrete and extreme example that came to dominate the news in the middle of 2021 made it impossible for me to ignore. It should also have been equally clear for anyone else to see.

At that time, there burst forth a widespread explosion of sympathy for the performer Britney Spears. Despite being an adult woman,

---

1   See Max J. Skidmore, *Presidents, Pandemics, and Politics,* New York: Palgrave/Macmillan, 2016.

and fully capable of enduring the stressful life of a successful performer who was earning a fortune, she had for years been subjected to overwhelming oppression by a conservatorship that empowered her father to control virtually every phase of her life. According to reports, the government had given him such power over her that he was able not only to take control of her money, but to deny her wish to remove an IUD. Thus, exercising the power he received from government, he forbade her to have a child. The outrage at the system that had stripped her of rights was certainly justified, and ultimately the court with jurisdiction ruled in her favor.

What would be equally justified would be a similar, and similarly widespread, outrage at anti-abortion legislation that subjects any pregnant person to a similar kind of oppression. What Ms Spears was *forbidden* to do, anti-abortion legislation *requires* women to do. Totalitarianism, or even a somewhat less invasive authoritarianism, works both ways. What government has the power to forbid, it can require; what it has the power to require, it can forbid. In either case, government has the power to control the individual, and strip away all powers of volition.

At first, my impulse was simply to comment on the injustice to Ms Spears, and to point out the related danger to an enormous segment of the population from anti-abortion activism—with repercussions that affect others who themselves do not or cannot become pregnant. After Ms Spears had testified, quite eloquently, on her own behalf, I prepared the following letter to the *New York Times*. *The Times* did not publish it. I regret not having submitted it elsewhere, or not having thought of other action at the time.

It is appropriate for this explanation to include the letter's substance here as my initial attempt at a public statement that a non-abortion case suggested regarding the dangers from zealous anti-abortionists:

To The Editor:

Many Americans are rightly concerned with the government's nearly totalitarian power over the talented performer, Britney Spears, who recently defended herself eloquently ("Finally Hearing From Britney Spears," July 2, A2). That power, she charges, demeans her, and has even prevented her from becoming pregnant.

The case of Ms Spears is a perfect example of what could happen to all women in the United States if Republicans gain full control. Despite being ostensibly against broad governmental powers, American "conservatives" would extend the power of the state to determine how any pregnant person must conduct herself; what she can do, or cannot do. Contrary to the rhetoric of those who profess to be "pro-life," this would instantly transform any person who becomes pregnant from a free citizen into a slave.

Outlawing abortion could be effective only if it subjected half the post-childhood population to complete governmental authority. Anti-abortion zealots should reconsider their positions, if they believe in limited government. The government that has the power to forbid abortion, under a different kind of authoritarianism, would have the power to *require* it, or, as in the case of Ms Spears, to forbid becoming pregnant.

As for my background, my wife and I at one time for several years were on the board of directors of a Planned Parenthood organization in a modestly-sized metropolitan area (she also volunteered there as an abortion counselor, and later, for some years she similarly volunteered for Planned Parenthood in a larger metropolitan area). Both these areas were in the Midwest. In addition to theoretical knowledge, I therefore have at least a touch of relevant practical experience that relates to the abortion issue.

Just as I had been thinking about the case of Britney Spears, a friend, knowing that I was widely published, and knowing that for more than a half century I had been a university professor teaching American politics, the presidency, and American political thought from all levels, undergraduate through doctorate, assumed that I would be reasonably well-informed regarding abortion.[2] He belonged to a rather large group of well-educated retirees who met regularly for presentations on current issues. Abortion was a topic that the group wanted to have scheduled, so in view of my background, he asked me to address them on the topic. I did so, after having crafted a somewhat comprehensive presentation. It was enormously well received, and contrary to my expectations, elicited no opposition.

Never one to let a good talk go to waste, I expanded it into an article. That article then became the nucleus for a deeper study that resulted in this book, *Abortion and Informed Common Sense*.

I proceed here with caution, and a sense of humility. A woman would be able to handle the subject far more personally. Men may certainly be able to appreciate a woman's desire to have a child. A man may even have the desire equally himself. It is doubtful, however, that a man could ever appreciate fully the horror a woman experiences who finds herself involuntarily pregnant and is in a situation of terror, such as abuse, abandonment, or extreme poverty.

Thus, any man who approaches the topic should do so carefully, with full explanation, and ever with consciousness of the need for humility. No man, or men in general, should be "The Decider" (as George W. Bush would have had it) of what a woman does with her reproductive system. Nor, in fact, should other women be in charge. Decisions on reproduction should be personal. Anyone

---

2   Max J. Skidmore, "Fire Bell in the Night: The Urgent Threat to Freedom From Anti-Abortion Activism," *World Affairs*, 185: 2 (June 2022)."

concerned about individual freedom, should immediately recognize that they *must* be personal.

This book takes note of the arguments against abortion. They deal with "life," fetal "heartbeat," the inevitable "killing," (ie, the "extinction of a human life"), and the ability to feel pain. I consider the allegation that at the moment of conception, a zygote is a "human person," that at all stages of development the growing creature, zygote, embryo, and fetus is a whole human being with the full range of human rights. Although the arguments tend to be framed in the guise of biology, I demonstrate that they almost never are truly based on science. Rather they reflect personal opinion, political ideology, or religious dogma often wrapped in a spurious notion of "personhood." I note that all these and other arguments overlook or dismiss any rights that the pregnant person may have, and that the "rights" that anti-abortionists assign to the growing organism supersede all other rights. The "rights" they assume at all stages up to birth take precedence over any rights possessed by individuals after birth. In fact, those who profess to be "pro-life" are obsessive about pregnancy, and *only* pregnancy (or pregnancy and birth); they have nothing to say about protecting life *after* birth. Almost never do they dilute their activities by becoming involved in such things as capital punishment, issues of war and peace, lethal police violence, firearms control, or the like.

Abortion and Informed Common Sense is the fourth in a tetralogy, of sorts. Each of the four deals with the application of common sense. A "common sense approach," to be sure, must be based on comprehensive knowledge. What may seem to be common sense, if proceeding from a position of ignorance, may simply be error reflecting a lack of understanding. Thus, when I refer to common sense, it must be understood that I mean "*informed* common sense," or common sense informed by adequate knowledge and accurate information.

"Tetralogy," to be sure, is not a precise fit. A purist would use "trilogy" to describe three related works generally of creative literature (novels, plays, operas, etc.), and "tetralogy," to describe four of these. Only one of the four discussed here, though, is a work of creative fiction, a novel. Nevertheless, because English has no other word that provides a better description, tetralogy seems to lend itself to an expanded definition. What we have here, then, is a work that adds a fourth volume that expands what I am calling a trilogy into a tetralogy.

As I described it elsewhere,[3] "In the United States, 'conservative' in contemporary usage denotes those with a general (often an intense) hostility to social welfare programs, dedication to low taxes (frequently rejecting the principle of progressive taxation), preference for a largely unregulated business community, and a romantic devotion to the Jeffersonian idea of localism and minimal government. American 'conservatives,' thus are closer in many ways to classical liberals than to true conservatives. Paradoxically, this does not prevent many of them from supporting authoritarian policies in non-economic matters."

Another characteristic of the American movement in recent years has emerged as a tendency to form a cult of personality around a revered leader. This began with a Republican devotion to the memory of President Ronald Reagan that became almost embarrassing to witness. Those seeking office, for example, argued that they would be "more like Ronald Reagan" than anyone else would be. Everything, at least rhetorically, had to fit into a Reaganite rubric, still framed through the "conservative" lens.

Then, in an even more astonishing manner, the conservatives' party, the Republicans, almost instantly transferred their obsession from the relatively refined Reagan to a new, openly crude, and far

---

3   Max J. Skidmore, "Review of C.C. Goldwater, ed., *Barry Goldwater, The Conscience of a Conservative*, Princeton: Princeton University Press, 2007 (originally published 1960), "*The European Legacy,* 13:5 (August 2008). P. 680.

more vulgar and unrestrained object, Donald Trump. Reagan virtually vanished from their collective memory as rapidly as Trump replaced him.

Similarly, the strongly ideological orientation faded, since Trump was too erratic and inconsistent to be a successful ideologue. Conservatism still informed their rhetoric, but the commitment to whatever popped into Trump's mind and tweeted out of his fingers became their guide, and his tweets defied prediction. Reagan had personified their ideology; Trump replaced Reagan, and even superseded ideology, leading the Republican Party in general to accept anything Trump did or professed to desire as their motivation.

Note, such obsessive idol worship is likely to be able to maintain such extraordinary intensity only for a while. Trump had asserted that he could "shoot someone on 5th Avenue and not lose a vote." What had seemed to be a joke began to appear almost literally to be true, when his "base" followed him regardless of inconsistency, or insanity.

A small crack in the stonewall of obsession, though, appeared in early 2022, when Trump told an audience that he had been vaccinated against Covid, had received a booster, and the audience should follow his lead. Some in the audience could not restrain themselves, and burst forth with "boo!" Apparently, they could accept murder on 5th Avenue, but not someone recommending that they care for their health (being reasonable would no doubt have been seen as too "liberal"). Along the same lines, a few Republican office holders began to argue that the party should look forward, not backward, and that Trump should cease his frantic efforts to overturn his electoral defeat.

This may be a sign that the blind adherent to Trump's whims will not continue after he fades from the scene. Reagan's symbolic importance for Republicans continued after his death. Adulation for Trump may die with him, since in contrast to their attitude toward Reagan, much of the Republican Trump reverence contains a significant component of fear; as much fear as admiration. The strange yet powerful reverence may not survive when he no longer is on the scene to punish and destroy.

As for the trilogy, it began with a recognition that although the movement that passes for "conservative" in the United States was growing, the conservative program does not work; it favors property rights over human rights, and if put into practice consistently fails to satisfy even its adherents. At first, I was not thinking of preparing a trilogy, let alone a tetralogy. After completing what became the first of the books, though, I knew that more should be done, and I knew that meant at least one more book, and perhaps more. There was a hiatus between the first one and the others, but the next two came quickly, both in the same year. They were followed soon by this, the fourth, completing what by now without doubt is a series; a tetralogy.

A number of other books currently are dealing with what must be called, with no exaggeration, an existential threat to democratic constitutionalism in the United States. The works of this tetralogy, however, are unique in that they are a whole, also dealing with the clear threat to democratic constitutionalism, but one that presents varied approaches, including synthesizing some other works, presenting comprehensive analyses and prescriptions, considering the situation in a brief, utopian novel, and then finally singling out a single, salient, issue that could, and should, be the motivating factor in 2022 that anti-slavery had become c.1860.

The first of the books, *Unworkable Conservatism*, came out in 2017. It looked at things as they are, rather than as they are professed by conservatives to be. The programs that conservatives advocate are extraordinarily difficult to implement, tend to be explicitly biased against the bulk of the population, and in the rare instances that they are put in place, satisfy no one, least of all those who advocated them. Remember "Let Reagan be Reagan"?

ABORTION AND INFORMED COMMON SENSE

It considers in depth eleven excellent works that deal with the corrupted state of American politics that has been almost entirely the fault of the Republican Party, along with the usual offenders, huge contributions that come from the ultra-wealthy—the malefactors of great wealth, that Theodore Roosevelt called them—that the Party aids and abets. It goes into some depth discussing the long line of malfeasance, including unpatriotic if not treasonous actions of the modern Republican Party, and decries mischief from the electoral college, while cautioning against putting much dependence upon the well-meant suggestions for reform that do not require constitutional amendment.

The second work, from 2020, is *The Common Sense Manifesto (With a Nod to Thomas Paine, Not Karl Marx)*. It examines the state of politics in America, tracing the recent history of the Republican Party and documenting the deterioration of its integrity, principles, and commitment to democratic norms. It describes a new form of politics and economics that will be essential if the political system is to be reformed. I call it Modern Political Economy, paying tribute to the promise from Modern Monetary Theory. It provides a "Common Sense Action Appendix," describing many reforms essential to overcome decades of deliberate corruption built into the system by those who seek to preserve the power of an elite minority, in cooperation with those motivated by religious fundamentalism who seek theocracy. In an additional appendix, it makes clear the descent of the modern Republican Party into open treason, working diligently to subvert popular government and bend the popular majority to its will. In a final appendix, it ventures into the unconventional. "Fighting is Wrong; Learn to Fight," speaks especially to women, but to others as well to encourage concern with personal safety, while yet encouraging engagement, civic action, and responsibility. This is so relevant to women that, with apologies, I decided also to reproduce it in this, the fourth, work, concentrating as it does on an issue potentially affecting almost any woman: abortion. Here, with some revisions, it becomes Chapter seven.

The third work is *It Can Happen Here: A Novel Look Backward*. This brief, utopian, novel, published also in 2020, by some three months preceded the election that cast from office a president who never should have been permitted to come near a position of power. It predicted much that would happen, but even it did not envision the desperate effort on the 6th of January 2021, to overthrow the Constitution, by force, if necessary, to keep that unfit president in power. The novel provides a glimpse of a future under progressive leadership, after thwarting an effort to prevent transfer of power.

I would have thought it preposterous to describe a violent attack upon the U.S. Capitol, with miscreants climbing walls, abusing law-enforcement officers, smearing excrement on what Americans long accepted as sacred spaces, stealing from the office of speaker of the House, constructing a gallows on the Capitol grounds, and openly seeking the vice president to kill and calling for the House speaker to be executed before the Trump-instigated mob. So, of course, I did not go so far.

The reality exceeded my imagination. Those things not only happened, but were televised in great detail for the entire world to watch. Republican officials, in as much danger as Democrats, cowered in fear in Capitol hideaways (while some members, traitors, tweeted clues as to their locations to the raging terrorists). For a few hours afterwards, all were traumatized, and many spoke of their fears, and of the hideous day of January 6th.

Presently, though—and suddenly—many of those very terrified officials, unable to withstand the shameless Trumpian lies, began denying that anything untoward had happened. Among the most notable was a new and especially obscure member of the House, Representative Andrew Clyde, a gun dealer from Georgia. During the January 6th insurrection, Clyde hid in terror, and was televised whimpering in fear for his life as he helped bar the door against the raging mob. A few days later, though, what may have been his natural belligerence returned. He aggressively argued that what television viewers everywhere witnessed with concern in real time, had, in fact, never happened at all; instead, it was a "normal tourist event."

January 6 was no coup attempt; absolutely not. Only "liberals" would call it a coup attempt. Rather than being a coup attempt, it was a time of celebration, of peaceful tourist tours through the Capitol. This was Clyde's mantra, but other Republicans were saying the same things.

For purposes of this book that looks at abortion, it is relevant to point out Clyde's duplicity, his habit of disregarding the truth. He is reported to have donated a building to a "crisis pregnancy center." These are agencies that promise to assist women with unwanted pregnancies to make informed decisions. Many women responding to their misleading propaganda come to them with the understanding that they present abortion as an option; they do not. Their real purpose is to pressure and bully vulnerable women and girls; to persuade them by any means whatever never to have an abortion. Their interest is not the woman; it is the fetus.

Compare Clyde's experience on January 6 with his later comments. Consider his contributions to an anti-abortion organization masquerading as an information center for women with unwanted pregnancies. Then make your own mind about whether he could be expected to tell the truth.

Open lies and denials about what they experienced, and about what the entire world saw, became the watchword of today's Republican Party. That party now continues on its merry way to suppress votes, subvert democracy, and attempt to ensure that women be stripped of their autonomy, and serve only as incubators for preservation of the human race, and for male pleasure.

Looking at abortion from the viewpoint of informed common sense is long overdue. This book provides that overdue look, along with my apology for not having given the warning sooner.

CHAPTER ONE

INCREASING THREATS TO REPRODUCTIVE RIGHTS

Two centuries ago, when the question of Missouri statehood arose, it introduced the subject of slavery squarely into the national political discourse. The potential danger to the Union was so great that Thomas Jefferson said it made him as fearful as a "fire bell in the night." He was well aware that the south's determination to continue to enslave human beings took priority over any other consideration.

The more astute readers of the *New York Times* should have been equally startled on November 7th, 2021, if they read the special opinion section carefully. That section contained suggested constitutional revisions that chosen contributors considered essential to permit America "to dream again." Most of the material was excellent, or at least would stimulate thoughtful consideration, but certainly not all.

One of the seven suggestions from seven scholars for a 28th amendment that this highly respected periodical—America's leading newspaper, one should note—selected to include, was poisonous; fully the equivalent of Jefferson's 'fire bell in the night." This suggested amendment would ban abortion except when "medical *certainty* exists" that a pregnancy would "cause the death of the mother" (emphasis added). It would mandate that the term "person" apply "from the moment of conception, at every stage of biological development, irrespective of age, health, function, gender, race or dependency."

Thus, the interests of the woman would barely be taken into consideration—grudgingly and only minimally—if, and only if, her life clearly and immediately were at risk. Her well-being, health, preferences, and even fundamental human rights would be cast aside as irrelevant—as would rape as a cause of the pregnancy. She would be reduced to the status of a vessel, or a slave.

The proposed amendment assumes the unquestioned truth of something that neither science nor common sense can support: a zygote, an embryo, or a fetus is equal to a fully-functioning, whole, human being (see Chapter Four for an expanded discussion). The Times has even seen fit to publish other op ed pieces making the same argument in successive issues.

Yet an embryo, say, cannot enable a taxpayer to receive a tax exemption, nor can it file for *habeas corpus* if inside an imprisoned woman, nor can a fetus. In a real sense, in fact, despite the abstract nature of embryonic "human rights," such an amendment would confer *extra* rights on a zygote, an embryo, or a fetus: the power to supersede and cancel any competing right held by a functioning, whole, human being. Such zealotry demands a response. Note that murder, *per se*, is not a federal crime, unless it is the murder of a federal officer. Murder is, of course, a crime, but it generally is punished only by a state, the District of Columbia, or a territory. The proposed amendment would make the killing of a fetus, an embryo, or even a zygote a federal crime; after gestation and birth, though, there would no longer be any protection from federal law. The proposal is an example of making an abstract superior to the concrete; of an obsession that excludes the practical. Little wonder that some people call anti-abortion activists "fetus lovers." That may sound harsh but it is true that they reflect no concern whatever for living, human beings; only for the fetus.

The history of abortion in the United States is not widely understood. Thus, misrepresentations abound, both unintentional and deliberate. Arguments against abortion tend too often to be accepted uncritically. The insistence that abortion is "murder," even though not widely accepted, has nevertheless framed the issue in a way that often affects the opinions even of many who disagree with the extremist formulation. It tends to make them express their disagreement in almost an apologetic manner. The effects of abortion restrictions, on the other hand, too rarely are recognized for what they always are, unconscionable violations of human freedom and dignity. Because of their skill in framing issues, the hypocrisy of many so-called "pro-life" activists tends to go unrecognized, and is almost never challenged.

For example, zealots tend to decry what they call the "abortion industry" as existing to reap profits. Their cleverly framed arguments tend to give them the advantage, obscuring reality. The reality is that under current conditions, there is no such thing as an "abortion industry" generating huge profits. To say that corporate profits are what motivate the demand for reproductive choice is utter nonsense.

Doctors who provide abortion tend to be highly dedicated. They have to be, because in order to provide abortions in America, a doctor must accept enormous personal sacrifices, including physical risk. Any physician in modern America could make far more money from any other kind of medical practice. Moreover, refusing to provide abortion would bring a doctor a huge side benefit: it would remove the constant threat of violent death. A doctor who performs abortions always is at risk of lethal danger from fanatic "pro-Life" terrorists bent on assassination, their fury excited by demagogic politicians or unscrupulous broadcasters seeking ratings. If the doctor does not perform abortions, the assassins would seek their targets elsewhere.

The proposed amendment, of course, is merely a proposal, but it reflects the extremism prevalent among Republican ranks, and especially blatant in the anti-abortion movement. It also reflects the obsession of extremists who trumpet their goal of saving every embryo. Realistically, that is impossible. Ignoring or misrepresenting reality—that is, lying—is the common thread of zealots, but rarely is it called out for criticism.

It is not extreme to say that pursuing anti-abortion policies leads to authoritarianism, to a climate of fear, as the recent legislation, Senate Bill 8, in Texas does. It makes abortions effectively illegal after an unrealistic six weeks. It enforces the prohibition by empowering citizens to be the enforcers. Anyone can bring a civil suit against anyone who performs an abortion, or has any connection to an abortion, regardless of how far-fetched that connection might be. The driver of a taxi or an Uber who—even unknowingly—drives a pregnant woman to a clinic for an abortion, for example, may be liable for a judgment of $10,000.

This enforcement mechanism places responsibility outside the state government, and is intended to avoid lawsuits against the state. The idea is that there can be no legal action against a state if no state official has performed an action. What it clearly does is to encourage citizens to spy upon, and bring suits against, other citizens.

Certainly, this is the modern, Texas, version of the infamous Fugitive Slave Law from 1850 that sought to make all citizens wherever located, agents of the "slave power." Under that law, if a southerner were to journey to a free state and present himself as an agent of a slaveowner, he could declare any person of African descent that he finds in that free state to be an escaped slave. The law then obligated every person in the free state, if requested, to assist the southerner in capturing, confining, and transporting the accused person to the south to be enslaved. If the local citizen refused the request to provide assistance in kidnapping the person of African descent, that refusal would constitute a felony.

In cases in which the status of the accused person were disputed, a commissioner would decide the fate of the accused. If the commissioner ruled that the accused person were indeed not an

4

escaped slave, that commissioner would receive a fee of $5. If the determination were in favor of the southerner's allegations, the commissioner's fee was $10. That passed for "fairness" when dealing with slavery.

Unquestionably the horrendous law helped bring on the Civil War (though in any case there were enormous forces, probably irresistible, already moving toward the bloody conflict). Echoes in modern times issue forth from those such as the junior senator from Texas, Ted Cruz, whom we hear speculating openly about secession. He warns, darkly, that it will be necessary if those who believe as he does fail to get their way. Such threats of treason have escalated because of Trump, but they are not new for contemporary Republicans. Trump, in the 2010 Nevada election for the U.S. Senate, for example, Sharron Angle, a failed Republican candidate, said that when election results do not satisfy "conservatives" they should resort to "Second Amendment remedies." This, of course, was before Trump was part of the political scene.

The parallel with the Fugitive Slave Law to be sure is not exact. Citizens now are not forced to bring suit. Anyone who chooses to do so, though—whether from sincere, anti-abortion motivation, greed, or pure malice—has legal authorization from the State of Texas to proceed. The plaintiff is rewarded only if the lawsuit finds its target to be "guilty."

The Texas state senator who claims to be responsible for Texas Senate Bill 8 set forth his rationale. Bryan Hughes wrote in the *Wall Street Journal* that he was the author of the Texas statute, saying that "The Texas Abortion Law Is Unconventional Because It Had to Be" (Sept. 12, 2021). He said that there was so much "ill-informed commentary" on what was termed the "Heartbeat Act," that it compelled him to "explain its provisions and defend its logic." The bill, he said (apparently with a straight face), "does not ban abortions after six weeks. It requires that a physician performing an abortion much first check for a fetal heartbeat," and that if a heartbeat is present, there may not be an abortion.

In fact, though, while there may be some electrical impulses, a flutter that at six weeks requires sophisticated instruments to detect, there is not yet enough of a heart to provide a true heartbeat. In any case, though, that should not matter. As we will demonstrate later, despite the obsession of anti-abortionists with "heartbeat," the actual timing of a real heartbeat is irrelevant.

For guidance one should rely on responsible medical sources, such as the Cleveland Clinic, that provide excellent material regarding stages of growth and fetal development; it is foolish to seek biological information from Texas state senators, or other anti-abortion propagandists. Moreover, most who become pregnant are not even aware of their pregnancies at six weeks. One may suspect that may be why the Texas law stipulates six weeks, so the legislators can deny that their law forbids abortion, while in practice making it almost impossible.

Hughes continues his explanation by stating personal opinion as fact: "the Supreme Court does not have the power to declare subjects off limits to democratically elected legislatures." The Constitution enumerates certain rights, he says, free speech, the right to keep and bear arms, "whereas the 'right' to abortion is a fantasy spun by the ludicrous logic of *Roe* v. *Wade*." Hughes is completely wrong.

Contrary to his dogmatic pronouncements the purpose of a constitution is to limit what government can do; to identify, establish, and protect rights. The Court does indeed have the power to declare subjects off limits to democratically-elected legislatures. Those rights, as the Ninth Amendmenta part of the Bill of Rights—makes clear, do not have to be specifically spelled out: "The enumeration in the Constitution, of certain rights, shall not be construed to deny or disparage others retained by the people," is the precise language.

Those rights may be group rights, or, as in the case of abortion, individual. The fact that Hughes says, "I believe life begins at conception, and I believe most Texans are in line with that understanding of human personhood," is immaterial. Why should anyone care what Hughes believes? Rights offer protections even from the understandings of majorities—or of zealots, even when elected; even when elected in Texas.

As shocking as the anti-abortion obsession is, the implications of the Texas statute are even more extreme. If the law is upheld, as appears likely, it opens the door to state nullification of any right that the Constitution of the United States guarantees. Governor Newsome of California has thrown it in the face of the Court that seems as devoted to its extremist (and NRA created) version of the Second Amendment as it is to overturning the right to abortion. He says that California will craft a statute based on the Texas law that will apply the same tactics to controlling firearms that Texas is using to ban abortion.

The common threat of all the new state laws on abortion is the desire to force women to carry pregnancies to term, regardless of their wishes, and usually regardless of their health needs. Numerous states under the influence of Republicans have adopted laws that will place complete, or almost complete, prohibition of abortion into practice if the Supreme Court overturns *Roe v. Wade*, and since the Republicans for decades have twisted procedures and packed the Court with anti-abortion ideologues there is good reason to believe that *Roe* will at best be rendered toothless if not completely destroyed.

The irony here is that the "partisan hacks" (to use a term that Justice Barrett employed to deny that it applied to the Court) that make up the right-wing ideologues of the Court's majority lied during their confirmation hearings. They professed their intention to adhere to precedent; or most preposterous of all, denied ever having thought much about abortion previously.

The Court in *Dobbs* v. *Jackson Women's Health* at this writing (January, 2022) is considering a Mississippi law that effectively prohibits abortions after the 15th week of pregnancy. It heard oral arguments on December 1, 2021. The law openly defies *Roe* v. *Wade* and *Planned Parenthood* v. *Casey* that currently set the Court's standard. No one can be certain regarding what the Court's action will be, but it bears repeating that Republicans have been diligent and disciplined in consistently adhering to their plan to warp the judiciary into an ideological force by packing it with right-wing extremists.[1] Their success has been impressive, but the contradictions and inadequacies of their "conservative" ideology has led their party to abandon their policy positions, disregard their duty to govern, and devote their energies solely to gaining and retaining power.

Consider the actions of Senate Republican leader Mitch McConnell. Not only did he slow confirmation of Democratic judicial nominations for years, but he declined to permit the Senate even to consider President Obama's nomination of Merrick Garland to the Supreme Court, holding the seat formerly held by the late Justice Antonin Scalia open for nearly a year, until Obama's Republican successor could fill it. McConnell's excuse was that vacancies on the Court should not be filled in a president's final year in office. When the president was a Republican, however, McConnell rushed to confirm any nomination, regardless of timing. In fact, as McConnell knew well, Justice Kennedy, who was sitting on the Court at the very time the majority leader was denying that justices could be confirmed in the last year of a president's term in office, was in fact confirmed in President Reagan's last year in office.

Contrast this with what happened when Vice President Agnew was forced out of office because he had accepted bribes when he had been executive of Baltimore County, also when he was gov-

---

1   See my *Common Sense Manifesto*, Washington: Westphalia Press, 2020, 192-198, for more extensive coverage.

ernor of Maryland, and also even when he was vice president.[2] Under the then fairly new 25th Amendment, a president has the power to nominate a new vice president to fill a vacancy in that office. Other presidential nominations, require confirmation only by the Senate; a nomination for vice president, though, also requires confirmation by the Senate, but in addition, and uniquely, requires confirmation the House as well.

President Nixon on the 12th of October 1973 submitted the name of Gerald Ford to be his new vice president. When Congress received Ford's nomination, it was generally assumed in Washington that the embattled Nixon was unlikely to overcome the Watergate scandal, and would surely resign or be removed through impeachment. They were correct. On August 8, 1974, avoiding impeachment, Richard M. Nixon became the only president ever to resign from office.

Ironically, Nixon's transgressions, the most serious in history up to that time, were minor compared to those of Trump. Trump actually inspired a violent coup against his own government, and against his own country's Constitution. He also, (thanks to the corrupted Republican Party's acceptance of the unacceptable) survived two impeachments.

Today, most Republicans continue to support Donald Trump despite being well aware of his unconstitutional efforts to overturn his electoral defeat. In sharp (and admirable) contrast, Republicans in 1974 joined Democrats in expressing their disgust at Nixon's crimes. Today, when called upon to hold Trump responsible for his considerably greater crimes, the official Republican position is to deny them vehemently, or simply to yawn.

Knowing that Nixon probably would not complete his second term, congressional Democrats could have refused to confirm any-

---

2   For the best treatment of Agnew, see the highly readable Rachel Maddow and Michael Yarvitz, *Bagman*, New York: Crown, 2020.

one he nominated to be vice president. If there had been no vice president when Nixon resigned, Speaker of the House, Carl Albert, a Democrat, was next in line, and would have become president.

Had they been as unprincipled as later Republicans proved to be, Democrats could have "stolen the presidency." They did not do so, even though it would have been easy. All they would have been required to do was to do nothing, but they declined simply to stonewall Ford's nomination (as McConnell decades later stonewalled Garland's). Democratic leaders supported Speaker Albert in declining to engage in such tactics. They recognized that a Republican had won the election for president, and they recognized that it would not have been honorable to go against the wishes of the voters. Democrats concluded that the voters had voted for a Republican, and therefore deserved to have a Republican as president. Contrast that with current Republicans who after the 2020 elections abrasively denied that the voters did what they so obviously did.

Joining the Republicans, the Democrats of both the House and the Senate voted to confirm Ford, who did, of course, become president when Nixon resigned. It would be completely futile to search for an instance of modern Republicans similarly putting honor above expedience on any issue, especially one that involved power—and most of all, for one that involved securing the presidency[3]

Currently we are more cynical and would likely dismiss all this by saying simply, "well times have changed." Indeed they have, but looking closely at how the times have changed, and why, it becomes plain that it is the degradation of the Republican Party, especially since the slash and burn tactics of the young Newt Gingrich, that instigated much of the change. Numerous works document this, most prominently Julian Zelizer's excellent study of what Gingrich wrought.[4]

---

3   See Skidmore, *Unworkable Conservatism*, pp. 136-137.

4   Julian Zelizer, *Burning Down the House: Newt Gingrich, The Fall of A Speaker*,

In spite of their professed admiration for The Founders, and their pious professions of dedication to "originalism," the Republican Party in 2020 and 2021 turned its back on one of America's greatest accomplishments, begun by one of its greatest Founders; a tradition dating all the way to Founder John Adams's defeat by Thomas Jefferson in 1800. When Adams recognized Jefferson as the legitimately-elected president, he ushered in centuries of willingness to accept election outcomes and ensure peaceful transfers of power.

To its everlasting discredit, however, following the defeat of its president in 2020, much of the Republican Party made its corruption plain, and attempted to retain that defeated president. The party professed to believe the unbelievable: the loser's preposterous lie that he really had "won by a landslide."

Violating centuries of sound—and essential—practice, Republicans accepted the lies of the poorest loser, and supported his inability to accept defeat. By refusing to convict him following his impeachment, they were complicit in his efforts to overturn the results of a fair election. Fundamentalist-evangelical "prophets" even convinced (and continue to convince) the gullible that a "miracle" will occur, and the disgraced and defeated president will be reinstated to office. That would indeed require a miracle. It cannot be done; there is no way under the Constitution that a former president can be "reinstated," except by being re-elected in a later election. Thus, even as there continues to be no reinstatement, defying the dates "prophesied," the "prophets" keep postponing the reinstatement date and the astonishingly gullible continue to accept these swindlers at their flawed word. Their gullible audience also continues to honor the dishonest pleas from the "prophets," to keep sending them more and more money. The preachers describe it, of course, as sending money "to the LORD."

As the Court moves to consider the Mississippi law, the anti-abor-

---

and the Rise of the New Republican Party, New York: Penguin Press, 2020.

tion propaganda campaign proceeds. An example was an article (December 14, 2021) in the *Kansas City Star* reprinted from the *Fort Worth Star-Telegram* (ironically, and appropriately, from Texas). The entire article was written as if any person reading it would have to be sympathetic to its message.

"She's Working 'To Save One Single Baby At a Time,'" was the gushing title. The author, Cynthia Allen, is a *Star-Telegram* writer who seems dedicated to spreading anti-abortion propaganda (another of her article titles is characteristic: "Texas Abortion Law is Already Saving Lives. But There is More to Do To Help Children").

In the article that the *Star* reprinted, she discussed Pat Pelletier, who with her late husband founded "Mother and Unborn Baby Care," a "crisis pregnancy center" 37 years ago in Fort Worth. Pelletier is president of the center that, in Allen's words, "has saved more than 9000 babies by offering women support and care as alternatives to abortion." Allen said that if the Court upholds Mississippi's law, it likely would be because of the majority's belief "that abortion policy should be left to the democratic process." The assumption is that democracy requires that, as Allen put it, the "horror of abortion" would no longer be accepted. Pelletier, she said, regarding abortion, looked to a future in which humanity will be unable even to imagine "that such an atrocity was allowed to occur with impunity."

Regardless of her opinion, or that of Texas state senator Hughes, fundamental rights must have constitutional protection; they cannot be subject to the democratic process, but rather must be protected from it. Majority opinion changes from time to time, and should guide public policy, but *not* at the expense of essential rights, no matter how unpopular a right may be at a given moment. When it suits their purposes, anti-abortionists are quick to disregard conflicts between constitutional rights and the democratic process.

Unfortunately, we now live in an age in which the extreme right denies science, and goes so far as to question the existence of facts, or whether it is important that a statement be true. They have referred to "alternate facts," meaning lies, as appropriate. This disreputable conduct is not new for them. More than a decade ago, in 2011, when he was a US senator from Arizona, John Kyle thundered that well over 90 percent of what Planned Parenthood did was, shudder!, *abortion!* The organization responded that Kyle's comment was simply not true. Only about 3 percent of its activities involved abortion. When questioned, a Kyle spokesman said something to the effect that what the senator said had not been "intended to be a factual statement." Well, no, it wasn't. He was merely caught in the act: the act of lying.

Those on the far right have little patience for science, except when they can pretend that it supports their ideology. They question the science of human-induced climate change, the science of vaccination, or the efficacy of masks to help prevent the spread of the virus that at this writing has led to the deaths of more than 800,000 Americans.

This in no way prevents them from citing "science" when they can twist it to support their positions, or when their misrepresentation makes it appear to render their positions support. Anti-abortionists, join with their right-wing allies and attempt to support their allegations by turning to—and certainly misrepresenting—science. Allen quotes Pelletier as "pointing to developments in medical science that are making it harder for people to deny personhood even at the earliest stages of life."

Despite their fervent belief, "science" does no such thing. "Personhood" is not a scientific fact. Rather, it is personal opinion, based on whatever criteria the observer chooses to consider as constituting a "person." Fundamentally, personhood is a matter of definition, not biology. Certainly a true heartbeat develops as a pregnancy continues, but that does not confer "personhood" on a fetus.

Any characteristic of a fetus that science can identify can also be found in a fetus carried by another animal. If any given characteristic—a heartbeat or whatever—confers "personhood," then any other animal with that characteristic would also have to be considered to possess "personhood." If not, then it is something else that science isn't identifying that constitutes a person. Heartbeat laws, therefore, are nonsense and are merely an excuse to forbid abortion. There is nothing about a heartbeat that is unique to a human being.

No anti-abortionist has accurately described any characteristic of a fetus—let alone of an embryo, or even less of a zygote—carried by a woman that science can show endows it with "personhood" to distinguish it from a similar fetus at a similar stage carried by any other animal. No one who professes to be "pro-life" and argues for "personhood" long before birth, would at the same time consider a fetus that any other animal is carrying to possess "personhood."

Anyone who attempts to use "science" to justify personal notions of "personhood," should also be made to explain how their "scientific" findings apply only to human beings. Saying, "well, only human beings have personhood," does not provide any scientific support for their belief, no matter how fervently held. Regardless of electrical flutters, or even ascertainable heartbeat, there is nothing science contributes to the important idea of personhood.

Surely, in assessing the extent of threats today to reproductive rights, a huge part of the threat comes from the U.S. Supreme Court. When hearing that we should never "pack the Court," it should be recognized that the word "pack" is pejorative; the Court has varied through the years, and nothing is sacred about its current structure. More to the point *the current Court has already been packed.*

Court "packing," thus can no longer be used as an argument against adding seats. Four new seats, or even six, are necessary to counter decades of Republican mischief. That mischief escalated when McConnell became Senate Republican leader, and culminated with

14

Donald Trump in power. He hurled nominations from the Oval Office for Senate leader Mitch McConnell to lead his Republicans in confirming. This was the McConnell who took the position that no Democratic president could be permitted to have a nomination confirmed, while any Republican nomination would be confirmed quickly and virtually without question. He used varied excuses not to consider nominations by a Democrat, depending upon the circumstances. Finally, though, he stopped making excuses, and simply continued his refusal to consider nominations from a Democrat.

As has been remarked, the Republican appointees, especially those from Trump, are doing precisely what they were nominated to do: come up with hard-right decisions, and move toward eliminating reproductive rights. Hard-liners Thomas and Alito already were on the Court. Gorsuch is similarly hard line, while Kavanaugh and Barrett take special pleasure in demeaning women.

Kavanaugh has a troubled history regarding women, and has mused aloud that perhaps the Constitution is "neutral" regarding abortion. Thus, he speculated, "perhaps the Court should be as well." Neutral means that judicial action would not be available to restrain states' most egregious actions regarding suppression of women. There is nothing even-handed about "neutrality," which accepts the most outrageous conduct as within the power of a state to impose.

Barrett is even more disturbing. She is a member of a quasi-Catholic fringe group, "People of Praise," so any criticism will be portrayed as anti-Catholic or as religious prejudice. Forget that. The group's principles and practices are dangerous. It adheres to ideas that can only be described as medieval at best. All involve submission of women. Barrett has had five children, and adopted two more. Requiring a woman to continue a pregnancy against her will, she says, imposes no hardship because after birth the woman can take advantage of "safe harbor" laws, and simply give the child away; therefore, no problem. Her statements are so suggestive of

15

the android women in the film "Stepford wives," that she could fairly be described as the first Stepford Justice.

The danger from the Court is real, but the Court at this writing (January 2022) has not yet acted. Predictions of Court decisions can be wrong. The dangers from the Texas SB 8 are real, and were already apparent at the end of 2021. The *New York Times* just after Thanksgiving featured a front-page article, "Texas Doctors Say Abortion Law Complicates Risky Pregnancies" (November 26, 2021). Even when a pregnancy is so troubled that it will ultimately endanger the pregnant woman's life and the fetus is certain not to survive, doctors are forbidden to perform an abortion—or even to recommend one—unless the threat to the woman's life is immediate. The law's supporters say their goal is to save every embryo, regardless of how the conception came to be. Thus, "embryo protection" is so overwhelming that it can even disregard child rape. The misogyny, and the fanaticism, here are so clear that they are painful to contemplate.

Sadly, by no means are they confined to men. Women can be equally fanatic and no less harsh. Take, for example, the comments of one Dr. Ingrid Skop, identified in the article as a San Antonio obstetrician who belongs to a group called the "American Association of Pro-Life Obstetricians and Gynecologists." In supporting the Texas law, Dr. Skop said that "even a girl as young as 9 or 10, impregnated by a father or a brother, could carry a baby to term *without health risks*" (emphasis added). The article quotes her as saying that, regardless of age, anyone who is sufficiently developed to become pregnant, can "safely" give a birth to a baby.

There you have it. Fanaticism is too mild a term to describe the core of the anti-abortion obsession.

Margaret Atwood, in her brilliant and horrible *Handmaid's Tale*, presents many outrages upon women in a society that, because of a pandemic, suffers from having too few women capable of becoming pregnant. Of course, this is a novel; it is fiction. Atwood says, though, that none of the outrages upon women that she describes are products of her imagination. Every one of them, she says, without exception, has happened to women sometime, somewhere, as a result of official policy.

Republicans where they can already are implementing many of them. More will come quickly. In many states where they are in the majority, Republicans are even attempting to secure legislation empowering their state's legislature to overturn popular votes for presidential electors. If a Democratic presidential candidate who favors abortion carries the state, for example, the legislature would be authorized instead to choose Republican electors who will cast their votes for the Republican, who opposes abortion.

Many professed "constitutional conservatives" believe the Constitution authorizes them to do this, and the infamous *Bush* v, *Gore* decision (2000) supports them. The ruling said that the Constitution grants state legislatures the full power to choose electors. The people themselves have no such constitutional right, said the Court, and "the Founders didn't give them one. Not only did the Court say that 'The individual has no federal constitutional right to vote for electors for the president of the United States unless and until the state legislature chooses a statewide election as the means to implement its power to appoint members of the electoral college,' but it made the point that the legislature can at any time go back on any promise it makes about choosing electors. 'The state legislature's power to select the manner for appointing electors is plenary; it may, if it so chooses, select the electors itself.' It can do so, even if it had permitted the voters to choose, but decided it doesn't like what the voters did."[5]

Republicans must be stopped. At all levels they must be stopped.

---

5   Max J. Skidmore, *It Can Happen Here: A Novel Look Backward*, Washington: Westphalia Press, 2020, pp. 25-26.

ABORTION AND INFORMED COMMON SENSE

This can only be done through the vote. It is vital to return Democrats to power in Washington and in the states and local jurisdictions as well.

Having said this, there are two glimmers of hope. On the 6th of July 2020, the US Supreme Court handed down a promising decision, *Chiafalo et al v. Washington*. At issue was the right of a state to bind presidential electors, to require that they vote for the candidates for whom they had been selected to vote. The Court almost unanimously held that states can, indeed, direct their presidential electors, and can replace them if they do not act accordingly.

Virtually all the commentary that I have seen centers on this right of states to fend off "faithless electors," who defy the state's wishes. Although *Chiafalo* does not mention overturning any part of *Bush v Gore*, and although I have seen nothing elsewhere that indicates this, it seems that Justice Kagan's opinion *clearly creates a right of the citizen to vote for presidential electors.*

Significantly, 8 justices signed on to her opinion, and Justice Thomas wrote a cautious concurrence. Her opinion for a virtually unanimous Court refers several times to a longstanding tradition, and to the duty of an elector to cast the "vote for the candidate whom the state's voters have chosen." The opinion, in fact, closes as follows: ". . . state election laws evolved to reinforce that development, ensuring that a State's *electors would vote the same way as its citizens.* Washington's law is only another in the same vein. It reflects *a longstanding tradition in which electors are not free agents; they are to vote for the candidate whom the State's voters have chosen"* (emphasis added).

If this is correct, the Court would reject any state's efforts to substitute its legislature's wishes for the judgment of its people. Of course, no one can predict a ruling, and the Court certainly is capable of being inconsistent, but it would seem that such a strong opinion would auger well for government by the people.

The other glimmer of hope is, perhaps, the brighter of the two. Medicine has progressed to the point at which medical abortions induced by drugs are simple, safe, and probably impossible to eliminate. It may be that, regardless of the current threats to abortion, and regardless of their strength in state legislatures, the anti-abortionists are fighting a losing battle. Abortion has never been eliminated, even in more primitive times. The notorious "back-alley," abortions, the equally notorious self-administered (and horrible) "coat hanger abortions" have always existed when the law forbids abortion. Medical abortions are far safer, and far more easily concealed, and thus the horrors may largely be avoided this time, even if abortions officially are all made illegal.

CHAPTER TWO

ABORTION IN AMERICA BEFORE ROE

T here is enormous lack of understanding about the history of abortion in the United States. Not only is there a shortage of information, but much that people believe they know is mistaken. As Will Rogers, and Mark Twain both are credited with saying, it isn't what people don't know that is so dangerous; it's what people *know* that simply is not true (or, as Will Rogers would have had it, "it ain't what people don't know that's so dangerous. It's what people *know*, that just *ain't so!*").

Until well into the 19th century, there were no restrictions at all on abortion in the United States, nor was there any stigma attached to ending a pregnancy before term. Abortion, as a rule, meant ending a pregnancy after "quickening"; early terminations did not even qualify ("quickening" was the time at which the pregnant woman first felt movement; that tends to be around the 15th or 16th week). The Roman Catholic Church itself then tended not to condemn abortion before that point. The argument was that a human soul did not enter the fetus until later in pregnancy; prior to that time terminating a pregnancy did not matter.

Even today, as Garry Wills points out, although the Church fervently condemns abortion, it does not argue that scriptures forbid it. The Church argues, rather, that abortion violates natural law. Wills is a superb scholar who is also a staunch Catholic, and who is fully familiar with thought on natural law. It would be unlikely to find a bishop or philosopher who could match his knowledge of the subject. Wills argues cogently in the *New York Times* (June 28, 2021) that the bishops, by forbidding abortion, are wrong on the issue.

As the 19th century progressed, there began to be efforts to curb the practice. This came about as there was gradual relaxation of restrictions on women, and almost assuredly was part of an effort to counter women's newly-found freedom. Consider, for one example, the development of the Post Office, however unlikely that may sound superficially.

As post offices emerged, they created incentives that encouraged women to leave their homes, unchaperoned, to collect the mail. Although postal officials made some efforts to segregate women from men to discourage mingling, they were unsuccessful, and the restrictions disappeared.

It is difficult to recognize today what a radical development—women leaving homes unescorted—that was, or how restrictive the culture tended to be. About a half century earlier, Thomas Jefferson reflected the prevailing attitude of the time when he wrote to Samuel Kercheval (September 5, 1816) that women should not vote because to do so would cause them to "mix promiscuously in the public meetings of men." That would lead to "depravation (*sic*) of morals and ambiguity of issue." It would be difficult to find an expression more demeaning to women than Jefferson's comment that their children, their issue, would be of uncertain parentage unless they, the women, were constantly confined to the home, or otherwise carefully supervised.

Opposition to abortion developed as part of a misogynist backlash that took place when women began to exercise new freedoms; any new freedoms. Change often is disruptive. That seems especially to be the case if change benefits women, and can be seen by men in any way as to their detriment.

To complicate the issue, both professionalism and economics became involved. Physicians began to organize as a profession. They sought to eliminate the widespread but often dangerous performance of abortions by persons who frequently were unskilled, and even untrained. These unskilled practitioners often were dangerous, to be sure, but also they always were in competition financially with the doctors. The doctors prevailed in their efforts to secure prohibitive legislation.

By the dawn of the 20th century, then, laws forbidding abortion had emerged across the United States. As is so obvious that it easily might be overlooked—the forest and trees phenomenon—men, without thinking it necessary to consult women, have always determined the substance of policy regarding abortion. That is, even though abortion is policy relating solely to women, women had no opportunity to participate in determining what the policy would be. To be sure, there have been improvements, but the new anti-abortion laws demeaning women—paralleled by laws as vigorously suppressing the votes from Black and Brown people as Jim Crow restrictions put in place following Reconstruction—are undisputed proof that this country still has many flaws that must be corrected if we are to begin to live up to the principles we profess, such as "liberty and justice for all."

The misogyny that inspired the early anti-abortion statutes was glaringly evident, but to be certain that it does not go unnoticed, consider the recent *Washington Post* op ed by law professor Aaron Tang.[1] He noted that the all-male medical lobby, as it campaigned against abortion, argued that a woman should not be permitted "to judge for herself" in such a matter, because women are "prone to derangement." It may be less open now, but the misogyny hasn't disappeared; it has only gone underground.

As the century progressed, despite the enormous damage done to women by abortion bans, they appeared to occasion little controversy. Perhaps this was attributable to reluctance of news media in those days to cover topics related to sex. So squeamish was the cul-

---

1   Aaron Tang, "Opinion: A Middle Ground on Abortion that Originalists Should Embrace, *Washington Post* (October 26, 2021).

ture at the time, that when first lady Betty Ford went public in 1974 regarding her breast cancer, it created a sensation. Both cancer and breasts were deemed unfit as topics of polite conversation. Ms Ford's courageous statements served to change the atmosphere, and to create a more realistic attitude regarding medical subjects.

Ironically, and perhaps paradoxically, this squeamishness had not prevented leering at women, comments about the size and shape of celebrity women's breasts, or jokes about "falsies." Popular culture was breast-obsessed, as reflected by the pointed, often padded, bras of the time.

To illustrate just how strong the preoccupation was in the 1950s, consider the reaction to the period's automobile styling. Cars had massive tailfins. They were laden with chrome, and protrusions sprouted forth on their front bumpers. Almost immediately, comedians christened those bullet-shaped additions to bumpers "dagmars." Dagmar was a buxom popular actress known for low necklines, tight sweaters, and large breasts. Winks and nudges were everywhere, but serious discussion was not appropriate for public discussion.

So perhaps it might have been expected that abortion—a serious topic and one not likely to generate humor—was virtually taboo as a topic. This changed, and changed dramatically, forced by a tragedy, during the early days of the Kennedy administration.

A new drug, Thalidomide, had become popular around the world as a sedative to help pregnant women sleep and to combat morning sickness, and for other complaints. Elsewhere, it often was available over the counter, but had never been approved for general use in the United States. It had, however, been approved for clinical trials, and had been widely distributed to doctors. That fact, suppressed at the time, has generally been forgotten.

The drug had been developed by a new, small, firm in Germany, *Chemie Grünenthal,* founded in 1954. This may or may not be relevant, but its top executives—like those of America's own post World War Two rocket and space programs, seem to have included large numbers of former Nazi officials, alleged war criminals, and high-ranking scientists who had advised Hitler. As corporate executives, they were thriving, just as rocket scientists fled and thrived elsewhere.

Here in the United States, on September 1960 during the waning days of the Eisenhower administration, the FDA had assigned the application for the drug's approval to Dr. Frances O. Kelsey, who was new on the job, but superbly qualified. She was both an MD and PhD pharmacologist. She considered the application from the American company who would market Thalidomide in the US, Richards-Merrell Pharmaceuticals, to have been inadequate. She knew that drugs often cross the placental barrier and might harm the developing fetus. She requested more information, over and over, only to be unsatisfied with the company's responses. The drug had never been tested to ensure it was safe for pregnant women to take.

Company executives streamed to Washington, condemning her to her superiors as a petty bureaucrat, and stubborn woman (a woman in a decidedly man's world, it should be noted) who unreasonably stood in the way of their marketing. I was in a management position then at the Department of Health, Education, and Welfare the predecessor of the Department of Health and Human Services. Although I was not in the Food and Drug Administration, I had some indirect knowledge of the exchanges, and of the pressure exerted on the "stubborn, fussy, woman." Fortunately, her superiors and the FDA in general, stood behind their new employee, giving her their complete support.

In early 1961, some reports from Europe intensified Dr. Kelsey's concern. The *British Medical Journal* published a report linking the drug to peripheral neuropathy. Indications from other reports suggested that users experienced shaking and numbness of hands. These reports verified her suspicions from the data she had seen, and caused Dr. Kelsey immediately to recognize the possibility that Thalidomide might harm a developing fetus. Shortly thereafter came an avalanche of information that made it clear that Thalidomide caused terrible birth defects. If taken in the first trimester of pregnancy, a prime time for morning sickness, the fetus would have damaged eyes, ears, bones, and hearts, and it caused missing limbs depending upon when in the first trimester the drug was taken. Even one dose was sufficient to cause horrific damage to a fetus.

What the company had called Dr. Kelsey's "fussy stubbornness" was actually the recognition by a skilled scientist that the evidence demonstrated that the drug was far from benign; that it unquestionably caused great harm. Her scientific insight helped to prevent the greatest human-caused epidemic of birth defects and childhood death in history. It also brought new legislation in 1962 that strengthened drug regulation, the Kefauver amendments to the Pure Food and Drug Act.

This is not to say, however, that the harm Thalidomide caused in the United States was limited to a few cases that involved drugs brought into the country from outside. Considering how much of the drug the company distributed for clinical trials, and how vigorously it was marketing it, the magnitude of the damage is likely to have been huge. Without Dr. Kelsey's deep scientific knowledge and obvious courage, that damage would have been far greater; an unparalleled tragedy.

On the 7th of August 1962, President John F. Kennedy awarded Dr. Kelsey the President's Award for Distinguished Federal Civilian Service. This was the highest award for a federal civil servant. Rather than being a petty bureaucrat who was damaging the interests of a commercial enterprise, she was acting as a courageous protector of the public who refused to be bullied. In other words, she was doing the job of a public servant.

In the meantime, a well-known figure in national children's television, brought the issue to the attention of a shocked public. Sherri Finkbine, who had four children already, was deliberately pregnant again. Her husband had purchased some sleeping pills in Europe, over the counter, and brought them home for her. They contained Thalidomide, and when she heard of the birth defects, she was concerned that her fetus might be harmed.

Abortion was her choice, but she found that it was illegal everywhere in America. Some states had laws permitting it to save the woman's life, but her life was not threatened. She sought an order from a court in Arizona, where she lived, permitting an abortion, and shielding her from prosecution. The court rejected her request. She discussed her situation with a reporter from the *Arizona Republic*, hoping to warn other women, but she could not secure permission for an abortion. She discovered that there was not a hospital in the United States where she could receive the procedure. The few that might have allowed it were frightened by the publicity. She was frantic. This was the situation that anti-abortionists want to restore to the country; women would have to seek "permission" yet still be denied abortions.

As a high status, white, woman she had privileges unavailable to most women in America, but that didn't matter. Women were forbidden to have abortions. She searched throughout Europe, and in August of 1962, she finally was able to have an abortion in Sweden. Swedish doctors verified that her fetus had been horribly disfigured, with missing limbs. Its chances of survival had been slim, and it could never have had a decent quality of life.

Few American women would have had the option to travel to Sweden. Even today, that would be expensive. At that time, international travel was far more expensive and less common than today. She was fortunate, but her status did not shield her from enormous anguish. Finkbine was to have two more children. Then, in a subsequent marriage, she became stepmother to another large family.

There should be no doubt that she was "pro family." There also is no doubt that her situation created a huge wave of sympathy. A recognition that harsh abortion laws were incompatible with human rights, brought a movement to repeal the draconian laws.

In 1973 (January 22), the U.S. Supreme Court handed down the landmark *Roe* v *Wade*. The Court declared that there could be no restrictions on abortion in the first trimester. In the second, states could apply some restrictions, but maternal health must have priority. In the final trimester, states could apply restrictions as desired, except that they must always permit abortion in cases in which reasonable medical judgment indicated that it was essential for maternal health.

Sarah Weddington, the very young lawyer who argued the case before the Court died in December (2021) at the age of 76. According to the *New York Times*, she had been a recent graduate of the University of Texas Law School, was only 26, and had never argued a case before *Roe*. She and her co-counsel Linda Coffee were representing Norma McCorvey (filing anonymously as Jane Roe), who was challenging the Texas law denying her an abortion. The opposing counsel, Jay Floyd, defending the law representing the state of Texas, The *Times* said, "opened the argument with what commentators have called 'the worst joke in legal history.'" He said, "when a man argues against two beautiful ladies like this, they are going to have the last word."[2] Despite the putdown, they did, but not with "feminine wiles," or whatever Floyd may have conjured up to explain his defeat; they overwhelmed him purely *by logic*. The Court ruled 7 to 2 to overturn the Texas statute.

---

2   Katharine Q. Seelye, "Sarah Weddington, Who Persuaded Court in Roe v. Wade, Dies at 76," *New York Times Obituaries* (Tuesday, December 28, 2021), p. A 20.

Weddington had previous experience assisting women in need of abortion. She had been part of a group of women who referred women to doctors who would perform them secretly, and illegally, or to doctors out of the country who would perform them legally. Although she did not reveal it until her 1992 book, *A Question of Choice*, she had an abortion herself. She and her boyfriend, Ron Weddington whom she later married, drove to Mexico where she had a safe abortion. She had been shocked at what women who did not have access to safe abortions would do to end their pregnancies, including eating dangerous chemicals, jumping down stairs, or beating themselves on their abdomens.[3] It is likely that these experiences enhanced her presentation before the Court.

The hysteria regarding abortion that solidified Catholic and fundamentalist/evangelical Protestant efforts to return to prohibition was soon to emerge. At first, the *Roe* v. *Wade* received praise, but after the rise of the religious right, said the *Times*, Weddington received death threats and had to travel with security.[4]

As is increasingly obvious today, the rise and virtual mainstreaming of the religious right and of right-wing extremism in general, along with the proliferation of firearms, and the constant repetition of preposterous allegations about "liberals" and Democrats has brought an avalanche of violence. For one example, one would think that any sentient being would immediately reject as absurd the charge that Hillary Clinton and Democrats in general were ringleaders in a pedophile ring out of the basement of a Washington, D.C. pizza restaurant.

Surely, no one could be stupid enough to believe it, yet one man armed himself and drove from North Carolina to Washington to fire off rounds in the pizza restaurant. He discovered only pizza, no children being abused, and not even a basement in the restaurant.

---

3   *Ibid.*
4   *Ibid.*

He went peacefully when arrested, saying that he guessed "the intel wasn't 100 percent."

As Dr. Frances Kelsey demonstrated, capable and conscientious public servants are essential. That should be obvious, but too often ideology overwhelms good sense. Her superb and fully professional performance indicated that almost two decades later, when President Ronald Reagan said in his inaugural address that government is not the solution, government is the problem, he was completely wrong. When he said the nine most terrifying words in the English language are, "I'm from the government and I'm here to help," he was speaking nonsense.

Government by quip or cliché is simpleminded, and a guarantee of bad government; so is medication by quip. However much one may believe that the immune system that nature gave us all will take care of everything, nature often needs assistance.

Similarly, those who oppose regulation, saying that the "free market" will take care of quality, that companies cannot produce dangerous goods because they could not survive, either have no understanding of how things work, or are being deliberately untruthful. *Grünenthal,* the marketer of Thalidomide, continued to exist.

Other companies, too, that have sold poisonous products causing mass tragedies, have survived unscathed. For example, in 1937, the S. E. Massengill Company dissolved a safe and effective anti-bacterial drug in diethylene glycol (DEG) to make it an oral medication. The resulting berry-flavored syrup killed over 100 people. The sulfa was safe, but the solvent was not; DEG had been known to be poisonous.

The company arrogantly refused to acknowledge responsibility, and continued in the industry. Even though the chemist who made the dreadful mistake creating the formula committed suicide, the cause no doubt was grief and guilt, certainly not the free market—and he was not a company executive.

Libertarian talking points lead to bad government and poor economics. The "free market," assuming that there is, or ever has been, such a thing, always needs assistance; a great deal of assistance.

Thomas Jefferson once complained of a "reign of witches," because of policies he rejected. There are strong forces today seeking to install a reign of witches, of sorts. They already have succeeded in the judiciary. They must be thwarted, the judiciary reformed, and the Court unpacked, and expanded in size. Otherwise, women are sure to be denied their right of reproductive freedom. They will be shunted back into the grim days of virtual enslavement.

CHAPTER THREE

THE DEVELOPMENT OF PROTESTANT ANTI-ABORTION ACTIVITY

A lthough the Catholic Church is known for its opposition to abortion, among rank-and-file churchgoers, the most zealous anti-abortionism these days seems generally to be among fundamentalist/evangelical Protestants. Despite a much longer history of opposition to abortion coming from the Roman Catholic Church, ordinary members have been inclined for many years (and for many reasons) to ignore the Church's teaching against contraception.

If it is correct that ordinary Catholics tend to be less concerned than fundamentalist/evangelical Protestants are about abortion, it may be that the American Catholic laity tendency to disregard priestly teaching about contraception may have led them to take teaching about abortion less seriously as well. After all, they may easily come to the obvious conclusion that contraception is certainly the most efficient way to reduce the number of abortions, so they may recognize the inconsistency in the Church's position. In any event, contrary to appearances, the history of Protestant activism against abortion does not go back far. It began relatively recently.

After Roe, States began to flood the Court with various attempts to restrict abortions. *Harris* v. *McRae* in 1980, upheld the Hyde Amendment that discriminated on the basis of income. The 1976 amendment prohibited federal funding of abortions, and states added their own prohibitions. Hyde first applied to the 1977 appropriations act, and has been renewed annually. There were some exceptions, and these varied through the years, but Hyde severely affected poor women who received care through Medicaid. It continues to have pernicious effects on huge numbers of women. That may soon become a thing of the past, depending on whether it remains in the budget bills Congress is considering. One can hope. It is noteworthy that President Biden (himself a devout Catholic) has called for the Hyde Amendment to be eliminated.

There were other relevant rulings. *Planned Parenthood* v. *Casey* in 1992 upheld a Pennsylvania law requiring a 24-hour waiting period, "counseling," reporting requirements, and parental consent. It did strike the provision requiring spousal notification (recognizing the possibility of an abusive spouse), and it added a new criterion, "viability."

There have been numerous other restrictions receiving the Court's approval. These are merely the high points (or low points).

Until later in the 20th century, though, abortion was not generally prominent in political discourse. As indicated, the most strident voices against abortion were Catholics. Protestants generally avoided the subject, or supported abortion. They generally considered it a "Catholic issue."

That changed when television evangelism emerged generating enormous fortunes, and when politics began to overwhelm religion among fundamentalist/evangelicals. In general, American fundamentalist/evangelicals had been likely to follow the biblical admonition to separate from the world, and thus often had not been active politically.[1] If they voted, they were likely to support the New Deal and later Democratic administrations because of Democratic economic policies (Republicans and fundamentalists had not yet succeeded in creating the nonsensical belief that Democrats are "agents of Satan"). In the 1970s and 1980s, though,

---

1   Max J. Skidmore, "Church and State in America: What Roger Williams Might Say Regarding the 2012 Elections," in Douglas Brattebo, *et al, The Presidential Election of 2012,* Akron, OH: University of Akron Press, 2015.

CHAPTER THREE: THE DEVELOPMENT OF
PROTESTANT ANTI-ABORTION ACTIVITY

there was what might be termed a new Great Awakening, of sorts. That revolved around the Calvinist teachings of Francis Schaeffer and his son, Frank, conservative Presbyterians who had returned to the US after years conducting L'Abri, a retreat in Switzerland. Schaeffer, himself, had been largely apolitical.

"Schaeffer's new stance reflected some of the philosophy of Rousas John Rushdooney, a twentieth-century Christian philosopher,"[2] and the most extreme of the evangelical/fundamentalists. He combined quasi-anarchist economics with a stark theocracy, and was the father of "Dominionism," or "Christian Re-constructionism." Broomfield writes that many scholars considered Schaeffer to be a dominionist, "as are Pat Robertson and even Sarah Palin," and he goes on to describe some of Rushdooney's ideas. Among them were his call for the creation of a Christian United States that would subdue the world. Rushdooney's agenda also included a huge expansion of the death penalty. Capital offenses would include not only those of today, but also adultery, blasphemy, homosexuality, the practice of astrology, incest, the striking of a parent, or "in the case of women, un-chastity before marriage." Broomfield says these "were a bit much for Schaeffer and Robertson," but he suggests that these and other leaders may to some extent have remained disciples who managed to make Rushdooney's doctrines "more palatable for the mainstream."[3] Nevertheless, he quoted Frank that his father thought Rushdooney to be "clinically insane,"[4] which seems to be a reasonable interpretation of one who, among other things, would put children to death for showing disrespect to their parents.

Frank writes that he and his father were the major force encour-

---

2   Charles S. Broomfield, *Francis A. Schaeffer: The Force Behind the Evangelical Takeover of the Republican Party in America*," unpublished M.A. thesis in political science, University of Missouri-Kansas City, 2012, p. 40.

3   *Ibid.*

4   *Ibid.*, p. 45.

aging American fundamentalist/evangelical leaders to become politically active, and to unite with those whom they had considered theological enemies. Specifically, Frank admits that he was the first to seize upon abortion as an important political topic that might energize evangelicals. Previously, as indicated, American Protestants had tended to dismiss it as a "Catholic issue." He described the making with his father of "a new Christian documentary titled *How Should We Then Live?*," a film that became a huge success "with the burgeoning religious right in America."[5]

As the younger Schaeffer described it:

> When we started making *How Should We Then Live?* Dad had not wanted to mention abortion in the series. We were already in production when the Supreme Court handed down the *Roe* v. *Wade* decision legalizing abortion. If it hadn't been for me, Dad's reputation as an evangelical scholar would have remained intact. As it was, my absolutist youthful commitment to the pro-life cause goaded my father into taking political positions far more extreme than came naturally to him.[6]

The elder Schaeffer said that he didn't "want to be identified with some Catholic issue. I'm not putting my reputation on the line for them!" he shouted. In words that would likely offend every fundamentalist/evangelical today, he raged in what Frank later called a shouting match[7], "what does abortion have to do with art and culture? I'm known as an intellectual, not for this sort of *political thing*."

Nevertheless, the father gave in. They changed the documentary, and

---

5   Ibid., p. 56.

6   Frank Schaeffer, *Crazy for God: How I Grew Up as One of the Elect, Helped Found the Religious Right, and Lived to Take it All (or Almost All) Back*, Cambridge: Da Capo Press, 2007, p. 260; quoted in Broomfield, p. 56.

7   Broomfield, pp, 56-57.

with it, they changed history. In 1977, thirty-four years after Francis Schaeffer began his ministry, the film appeared on the market. It was a sensation. Now, after nearly a half century, it remains available. Through the years it has sold millions of copies, and "it became a staple of evangelical/fundamentalist" teachings for Protestants and Catholics as well.[8] Abortion became the key issue uniting the religious right as they rage not only against the modern world in general, but specifically against the government of the United States. The Schaeffers had framed their issues so powerfully that they overcame the traditional enmity between Protestants and Catholics, especially between Baptists and Catholics. Without the issue of abortion—a political issue masquerading as religion—it is doubtful that the disparate elements of the religious right in America would have been able to merge into such a powerful political force, one that today is seriously presenting a fascist alternative as a threat to the democratic republic, and to the very idea of self-government.

Frank now admits with regret that the group that he and his father worked with and influenced so strongly, "such evangelical/fundamentalist luminaries as Jerry Falwell, Pat Robertson, Franklin Graham, James Dobson and John Hagee" were a "hate-America group," and that he and his father crossed the line into open sedition. He and his father not only were part of this group, but were leaders. "We were very anti-American," Frank said. "We became a truly anti-American force."[9]

The Schaeffers had become openly political, and therefore were eager to spread their influence beyond explicitly religious circles. In the 1970s and 1980s they met frequently with such powerful political figures as Ronald Reagan, George H. W. Bush, Gerald Ford, Jack Kemp (who was the Republican candidate for vice president in 1996), and then Surgeon General C. Everett Koop. Frank said

---

8   *Ibid.*, pp, 57-58,

9   *Ibid.*, pp. 8-9.

that "the evangelical antiabortion movement that Dad, Koop, and I helped create seduced the Republican Party."[10] Before the Schaeffers, Frank said speaking of politicians, "nobody paid any attention to Jesus" until "Kemp, Koop, and Reagan realized that they could pry off Catholics' and evangelicals' votes from the Democratic Party." As it is now, he said, "religion in America is politics . . . big-time politics."[11]

Remember, all this was decades ago. The Trump phenomenon was in the distant future. When it exploded on the scene, though, it overshadowed even the Republican Party's recent patron saint, Ronald Reagan.

Melding together the evangelical and conservative political communities, the Schaeffers became "evangelical/fundamentalist royalty" in America. Jerry Falwell helped spread their writings throughout the congregations of the religious right. They "became fixtures in the Christian Right community," and were invited constantly to speak at churches, on Christian radio, and on television shows across the country. "Frank speaks at length in *Crazy for God* about their many personal experiences with Falwell, Robertson, Ralph Reed, [Tim] LaHaye, Dobson, and many others."[12]

Francis Schaeffer's final book, *A Christian Manifesto*,[13] was among his most thorough and influential statements. It was here, and in his sermon the following year, 1982, at the Coral Ridge Presbyterian Church in Fort Lauderdale, where he cast aside any pretense of moderation. He recognized that he was dealing with dangerously subversive issues, but he persisted.

In his lengthy sermon, he contrasted the "Christian world view"

---

10   *Ibid.*, p. 76.

11   *Ibid.*, p. 9.

12   *Ibid.*, p. 75.

13   Francis Schaeffer, *A Christian Manifesto*, Westchester, Illinois: Crossway, 1981.

with that of the "humanist," which he said saw man as the measure of all things. The latter grew from "Darwin's theory of evolution, which fundamentalists had hated since Darwin proposed it in 1859." He railed against the wrongs that he and other fundamentalists saw in America, "permissiveness, pornography, the public schools, the breakdown in the family, and finally abortion." He saw recent Court rulings—dealing with prayer in public schools, religious symbols on public property, and abortion—as stripping Christians of their "freedoms." "It was Schaeffer who led the way for evangelical/fundamentalist Christians to begin thinking that American democracy had been established by Christians and that the Declaration of Independence and the Constitution had been written" by the Founders deliberately to establish a "nation based on the Judeo-Christian ethic" and a "literal interpretation of the Bible."[14] Only one word, he thundered, could describe the United States of today: "TYRANNY! TYRANNY! That's what we face," he roared.[15]

Certainly, Frank Schaeffer rejected, and now regrets, his past and his role in inciting political extremism in America. He describes his awakening in *Crazy for God: How I Grew Up as One of the Elect, Helped Found the Religious Right, and Lived to Take it All (or Almost All) Back.*[16] He had become increasingly uncomfortable, not only with what he was doing, but with the people with whom he was associating. "His devotion to the arts ran counter to much that he perceived among the Schaeffer followers in the U.S." Finally, "he came to recognize that the forces he unleashed were deadly. Among the most extreme were Rushdooney's Christian Reconstructionists," including Rushdooney's son-in-law, Gary North—who began the Christian homeschooling movement. Many of these, North included, have ties to the right-wing extremist John Birch

---

14   Broomfield, p. 43.

15   *Ibid., p. 44.*

16   Cambridge: Da Capo Press, 2007.

Society that once was so prominent on the far right that it seemed to represent all its varied elements. Reconstructionist doctrines also have adherents among the 'C Street Group,' or 'The Family,' in Washington, D.C., that includes powerful politicians, predominantly Republican but also some Democrats. The younger Schaeffer also noted the violence in the anti-abortion movement, and the "anti-government rhetoric on the right that at least flirts with revolution and secession." Regardless of the "flag-waiving veneer of patriotism" there was a "stark hatred for America, for democracy, and for the American political system. His journey away from fundamentalism began when he was startled to recognize that, in the land that his followers hoped to create, he would be among the first to be eliminated."[17]

The violent attempt by Trump followers on January 6, 2021, to halt the counting of electoral votes was a clear attack on America's system that places voters at the center of public policy. The insurrection attempt, and the current advocacy of voter suppression that is quite open among Republicans, is the flowering of those seditionist seeds planted by fundamentalist/evangelical anti-abortionists decades ago. They opposed democracy then, and they are at least equally opposed to democracy today, as they have taken pains to demonstrate. Their ferocity should have been expected.

Frank Schaeffer recognized a core influence that he perceived in all fundamentalisms of the world, "whether Jewish, Islamic, Christian, or some other: a hatred of women, and of sex, all under the guiding motivation of fear; hence, his sub-title: "How the Bible's Strange Take on Sex Led to Crazy Politics—and How I Learned to Love Women (and Jesus) Anyway." He draws an indirect "but deadly connection between the 'intellectual' fig-leaf providers and periodic upheavals like the looney American Right's sometimes vio-

17   Max J. Skidmore, Review of *Sex, Mom, and God*," *Journal of American Culture*, 35:2 (June 2012), pp. 198-199; see also Jeff Sharlet, *The Family: The Secret Fundamentalism at the Heart of American Power*, New York: Harper, 2008.

lent reaction to the election of people like Barack Obama." He said that of course "your average member of some moronic gun-toting Michigan militia is *not* reading Francis Schaeffer." What the Religious Right's "Roman Catholic and Protestant enablers" did do was to raise questions of legitimacy and illegitimacy that sought to create doubt about "the very legitimacy of our government."[18]

If there were any question that the younger Schaeffer was prescient in his urgent warnings, the attempted insurrection on the 6th of January should remove all doubts. We now are at a junction. The established order in this country faces a large armed and vicious minority sharing a commitment to violence, and openly advocating the elimination of democratic procedures, flirting with secession, and held together by a mutual misogynistic horror regarding abortion, leading them to delusions of Democrats as literally agents of Satan.

---

18   Skidmore, *Ibid.*

CHAPTER FOUR

HOW ARGUMENTS AGAINST ABORTION ARE WRONG, WHY LANGUAGE IS IMPORTANT, AND HOW FUNDAMENTALISM IS PERILOUS

The first thing to consider is language, and whether arguments against abortion actually make sense. Careful scrutiny reveals that they are based far more on emotion than on reason.

Those who control, or strongly influence, the way people speak—hence, the way people think—have a major advantage that is difficult for others to overcome. It is urgent, therefore, to be careful about language usage. Referring to tax cuts as "tax relief," for example, implies that the overall tax levels are greatly burdensome, even if the speaker had no intention of saying that. The fact is that American taxes on the affluent are considerably lower than those in most advanced, industrial countries. This is true, even when considering all taxes together, state, local, national, and going so far as to include Social Security.

People who think of tax reductions as "tax relief," however, are conditioned not to recognize that, and not to appreciate that they get services in return for those taxes. Actually, many countries tax more and provide far greater benefits to their populations than America does. Generally their citizens—who are not constantly inundated with anti-tax propaganda and condemnation of social programs—consider it to be a good bargain.

It is equally misleading, and no doubt deliberately so, to include Medicare and Social Security as part of a "safety net." That term im-

43

plies the existence of a program to catch people falling into poverty. Social Security and Medicare are social insurance programs, into which people pay, and from which they receive benefits when they qualify. They do not require that beneficiaries demonstrate poverty. Nearly all Americans qualify, thus it is appropriate to describe these programs, for all practical purposes, as universal. Recipients recognize that these programs provide them with earned benefits, not means tested "welfare" for the poor. Referring to them as parts of a safety net may create the assumption that they are charity, or unearned benefits, thus making them more vulnerable to political attack from opponents.

Another dangerous term that nearly everyone uses who discusses reforming our politicized federal courts is "court packing." The term dates back to Franklin D. Roosevelt's 1937 attempt to change the composition of the Supreme Court by adding seats to compensate for those held by justices who were under the influence of an outdated political ideology. Opponents of FDR's move called it a "court-packing" plan, and the term continues to dominate the discourse, even though it clearly implies something sinister. In FDR's case, the Court ultimately retained the same number of seats, but its rulings became more favorable to the administration (and to the people, who overwhelmingly supported the administration). FDR, in fact, considered himself to have won the war, even if he lost the battle. In any case, a number of retirements soon made it the Roosevelt Court, and rendered any changes unnecessary.

The situation today is far different. The entire federal judiciary, not merely the Supreme Court, suffers from decades of extremist appointments by conservative presidents, and from unwillingness of the Senate when Republican controlled to permit less conservative presidents to fill judicial vacancies. The judiciary needs to be "unpacked."

This packing that clearly exists today came during a time when Democrats received far more votes than Republicans, both for the presidency, and for members of both houses of Congress. Consider, for example, that of the last eight presidential elections, Republicans won the popular vote only once, and that the great majority of US senators represent states with relatively small populations, thus making them always represent far fewer voters than those from more populous states. This hardly reflects "democracy."

Part of the explanation of how this happened is that—in addition to the constitutionally-mandated structure that now enables a minority of the population to choose a majority of the Senate. Senate conservatives for decades implemented and jealously protected rules to empower conservatives even when they are in the minority. In truth, then, Court "packing" has already taken place.

The Court is dominated by a two-to-one majority of justices chosen deliberately because they are hostile to abortion (although none of them admitted that during their confirmation hearings). The Court appears ready to rule that states are free to restrict abortion as they wish. Reform of the entire judiciary is essential, most notably at the appellate level, including the fifth, sixth, seventh, eight, and eleventh circuits. Reform of the Supreme Court is especially urgent, and should be done before the packed Court acts to remove constitutional protections for women's right to abortion. Whether that is possible with only 50 Democratic votes is questionable, since one of them, Senator Manchin of West Virginia, is openly a conservative, and another, Senator Sinema of Arizona, is openly subject to inconsistent and apparently irrational whims.

Conservatives now are openly attempting to employ measures to thwart the will of the people; for example, by working to empower state legislatures dominated by Republicans to cancel votes when they do not like the outcome of elections. Government by the people requires a judiciary not filled with (as Justice Barrett put it) "political hacks"; one that will prevent, not protect, efforts to trample majority will while at the same time preserving individual rights. Continuation of our democratic republic requires measures to *unpack* the Court. Thus, adding four to six seats to the Supreme Court should be described as Court reform, or even, to reiterate, "Court unpacking."

"Pro-Life," is another salient example. Everyone favors "life," in general, but the anti-abortion movement has appropriated a general term and applied it to a quite narrow subject. The movement does not apply the term elsewhere, only to abortion. "Pro-life" has become their synonym for "anti-abortion," and *only* for anti-abortion. Forced Birthers would be more appropriate.

It certainly does not apply to police reform, saying nothing about the wave of killings by police (most often of Black men) following traffic stops for minor violations, or the other instances when the first inclination by police to handle a situation is to reach for firearms, rather than to de-escalate. In December 2021, for example, Los Angeles police killed a 14-year-old innocent bystander who was in a changing room in a department store. The police had been called because a disturbed man had attacked patrons. The police shot and killed the offender, but their bullets also injured—and killed—people who were not involved, going through a wall to kill the young woman trying on a dress.

What was the offender's weapon? A large bicycle lock! What happened to police training, when officers no longer can overcome an unarmed target without blasting away? Where are "pro-lifers" when there is something so manifestly wrong, and so destructive of human life?

"Pro-life," then, is a fraud, a clever sleight of tongue that becomes a sleight of mind. To anti-abortionists the term never suggests actual concern for life, itself, only for the protection of a fetus, an embryo, or even a zygote or a stem cell. To belabor the point, "Pro-Life" does not include opposition to capital punishment. Nor does it suggest opposition to war. Certainly, anti-abortionists do not use it to oppose the widespread public availability of instruments of war such as rapid fire, high capacity, firearms that are designed to kill human beings quickly and efficiently. Nor do they apply it to support the provision of universal life-saving health care, or for adequate food or shelter.

The appearance of plausibility to anti-abortion arguments and other terms, like the implications intended by the term "pro-life," is equally misleading, and completely superficial. At the risk of being misunderstood and misrepresented it is important also to consider the word "kill." Anti-abortionists—only when speaking of abortion of course—use it as though it always, without question, denotes something horrible. Certainly, "killing" can describe monstrous acts, but "killing" can be terrible, or relatively benign, depending upon the thing being "killed." Plucking a pear from a tree elicits no sympathy for the pear; nor does digging up a potato cause sympathy for the potato plant from anyone.

Conservative writers stress that abortion "kills." Catholic conservatives, it seems, most often argue thusly, and they often achieve their desired response. Interestingly, although the Church opposes capital punishment, Catholic anti-abortionists rarely seem to make that an issue. They tend to get considerably more upset about the status of an embryo or a fetus than about an adult in a death chamber. Surely, that reflects the influence of the political issues of the day, and they may be acting on that influence without even being aware of it.

Undoubtedly, Catholics opposing abortion resort to the argument that abortion kills in order to put those who favor reproductive choice on the defensive; they use it because it often works. "No one can deny that abortion 'kills,' they say." This is true in a literal sense, but it definitely is not true that it must be accepted that the "killing" described is the taking of a human life. Nor must one accept that such an argument, *even if it were true*, destroys any right whatever to abortion.

47

However one attempts to define "killing," people who believe that killing, *per se forbids* abortion should recognize also that they must approve enormous power to government officials: the power to supersede all rights of a pregnant woman. Giving government such power forces her, regardless of circumstances, to continue a pregnancy to term against her will.

No one has the right to make such a demand upon a woman any more than it would be acceptable to require her to sacrifice her life against her will to save a fetus. It would also be unacceptable to *require* a woman who wants to bear a child to undergo an abortion.

As a matter of fact, life exists *because* of "killing." Even vegans depend upon the killing of plants to survive. Health often requires the killing of bacteria, either through the body's natural defenses, or through the action of antibiotics. Self-protection may require the swatting, the killing, of a mosquito. Rarely would anyone think of this as horrible, although if mosquitoes were to have a point of view, they no doubt would disagree

The use of the word "kill" when applied to abortion literally means different things depending upon timing: the more distant the birth, the less force the word should have. Conservatives here, as in so many circumstances, tend not to be consistent. They call for legislation to prevent termination of a zygote or an embryo, but reject calls for gun control to prevent the mass killing by firearms of whole, functioning, human beings.

Massacres, they often say, require merely "thoughts and prayers." Oddly, they never seem to recognize that gun violence will continue, regardless, so long as firearms remain so available—that is, so long as policymakers refuse to control them. They also never rely on "thoughts and prayers" to prevent other crime. They believe laws are required to deal with the fraudulent votes that (despite convincing evidence) they are so convinced exist anywhere that Republicans lose elections. They do not think they can do without walls to keep out others they believe should not come into the country. Nor do they rely on thoughts and prayers to eliminate abortion, preferring the much more effective use of coercion. Apparently, thoughts and prayers are limited in their application only to massacres with firearms.

The "unborn child" is a phrase virtually universal among abortion opponents, and mischaracterizes the situation entirely—and, of course, deliberately. No one argues that a child is an adult. There is no more reason to say that a fetus is a child, nor that an embryo is a fetus, nor that a zygote is an embryo—let alone a child, or even an infant. There are differences. Children and adults are fully functioning, whole, human beings. Zygotes and embryos are not, nor is a fetus, especially early in a pregnancy. The important developmental phase is not the heart, it is the brain and nervous system.

The question of "life," is also designed to close out any argument. There is no question that in a pregnancy life exists in the womb, but life exists in every cell throughout the body. A cell anywhere in the body is alive, yes; that also is irrelevant. A banana slug is alive; so is a penicillin mold or a growing turnip. No one suggests that they should have the rights of human beings. It is erroneous to conclude that "life" implies "human life," or even that "human life" means the same thing when applied to a zygote or to an adult—or to a child. It is more a matter of definition than of biology. The point at which a developing fetus becomes capable of functioning as a whole human being outside the womb, viability, depends upon brain and nervous system development, and certainly is late in a pregnancy, close to birth.

Consider the other end of the human life cycle. When a human being's brain ceases to function—when there is no more cognition—that human being may be taken off life support, so obviously is not accorded the full rights of human beings, even though without question a whole human being with rights had previously existed. That brain-dead person remains "human" biologically, but only biologically, not in the sense of function or sentience.

Similarly misleading, and deliberately so, is the question of fetal heartbeat. Anti-abortionists make dubious assertions that "fetal heartbeat" takes place quite early in a pregnancy. Even if that were true, it is another irrelevant factor.

We have a tendency to romanticize the "heart," but when our vocabulary does so, it sacrifices accuracy for style or beauty; one might say for poetry. Romantic love, for example, clearly relates to the brain, stimulated by sensations and hormones, not the heart. A beating heart certainly is not exclusive to human life. Except for some simple sea creatures, all animal life (including a banana slug) has a heart, and all hearts beat. A beating heart does not imply that the being must be accorded human rights—or animal rights, for that matter. If it did, an octopus would have triple rights; each octopus has three hearts. Nor are stem cells from human beings "tiny little humans," as some ideologues have fantasized.

Conservatives frequently become carried away by abstractions so extreme as to be ridiculous. An argument can begin as intelligent, but get so convoluted and unrelated to reality that it becomes simply stupid.

Some years ago, arguments swirled around the "rights" of stem cells. Former Republican senator John Danforth, who is both a clergyman and a lawyer—and who, despite his benign reputation, is strongly partisan—he is the one, after all, who gave us Clarence Thomas on the Court—pointed out the absurdity of the argument. If rescue personnel were in a burning house and could rescue only a person, or a dish of stem cells, he said, there would be no question that the person—a functioning, whole, human being—should be saved, not a dish of simple non-sentient cells. Such a dish of cells could be spread throughout the room by a sneeze.

However, a reporter subsequently asked Missouri Republican Senator Jim Talent, then running for re-election, which one, under such a circumstance, should be rescued. Talent apparently was not a stupid man, but his response was ridiculous: the rescuer, he said, would have to ponder the morals, and accordingly make a decision on the spot: "Hmmm. Should I save the stem cells, or the person?" That may not have caused Talent's defeat, but certainly did not increase his chances of re-election.

There is another argument that abortion opponents would consider key, that others would not. Admittedly, it is completely a matter of judgment.

Abortion prevents a human life from becoming possible from a given pregnancy. That certainly is true, but it also is an argument against effective contraception. Here, though, is where an argument that might initially seem compelling becomes so abstract as to be meaningless. Both abortion and effective contraception may prevent a complete human life from developing, but is that really compelling? *It is equally an argument against abstinence, and in favor of forced, and involuntary, pregnancies.* Regardless of how that might be rationalized, it is completely unacceptable.

Even those who oppose contraception would be unlikely to argue—and it would be an absurd argument—that human beings have an obligation to engage constantly in unprotected sex. It would certainly be rare to hear such an argument: "a couple—or even any man and any woman—should engage in sex whenever together, because to refrain from doing so would prevent a human being from developing." Anyone would recognize such an argument as absurd, but is it really much different from arguing against contraception, especially if the one making the argument also opposes abortion?

I have a friend who is opposed to abortion, because his grandmother had been raped. Had she undergone an abortion, he would not have been born. True. Is this, though, a valid argument? If it argues against abortion, it also argues against contraception (but of course that is irrelevant to many anti-abortionists, who also are opposed to contraception). Even more important, it argues against abstinence—*and even justifies rape.* Again, such an idea is morally indefensible

Regardless of any merit to any of these arguments, they fall apart completely when a rational person of good will notices that they ignore an enormously important part of the consideration. Whatever the definition applied to any stage of development, there is complete lack of concern for the woman involved. She is essential, but she is treated as irrelevant; she is unimportant except as a vessel.

Even if it seems tiresome to repeat it numerous times, it is essential to recognize that *all anti-abortion arguments completely ignore women and their* rights. One should remember that women, half of humanity, also are whole, functioning, human beings and thus should have control of their own bodies. That is, they have rights, just as men do, just as all human beings do. Women's rights certainly are at least equal to any "rights" that ideologues may assume belong to an embryo or a fetus. Similarly, women's rights are in no way inferior to the "rights" of male-dominated policymakers who presume to require a woman to continue an unwanted pregnancy against her will, or to become pregnant when she wants not to do so.

Regardless of the implications of the arguments of those opposing abortion, they are unlikely to argue openly that women should have no rights. In fact, many anti-abortionists attempt to argue the impossible: that by opposing abortion, they actually are protecting women's rights; in an Orwellian twist, they may actually have managed to make themselves believe what they say.

The only people who would argue openly that women have no rights, and moreover, that they *should* have no rights are likely to be found in the viciously insane ranks of "incels," the involuntarily celibate. These are warped men who cannot find willing female partners to engage in sex, and who therefore hate women because they irrationally believe that women have an obligation to service them, regardless of the women's own wishes.

Finally, there is an argument anti-abortionists use regarding pain. It is seemingly definite that, considering the developmental status of the nervous system, pain perception could not exist during the first two trimesters. Nevertheless, it is well to be skeptical when experts give assurances regarding things that it is to their advantage not to have to deal with.

I remember vividly an instance of infant circumcision, decades ago. The parents, a young and anxious couple, received assurances from the obstetrician who was to perform the procedure on their month-old infant, that there was no need for anesthesia or even analgesia, because such a young infant would not feel the brief surgery. They were on a floor below waiting until it was completed, when they clearly heard the infant's anguished scream. The husband said he wished he could have "decked" the uncaring obstetrician.

Nevertheless, there now should be no issue regarding pain during abortion. Whether necessary or not, current pain-suppressing medications are quite highly developed. Regardless of whether they actually are needed, as a precaution they can, and should, be administered routinely, especially for later-term abortions.

As for rights, a reasonable interpretation would be that the *woman's* rights, as the sentient being most intimately involved, should *supersede* all others. Implicitly, advocates of a "personhood amendment" to the Constitution may be at least vaguely aware that the Constitution may support a woman's rights. They recognize that if the Constitution as it exists *does* provide rights for women, it thus will sanction abortion. They are conceding that it may be impossible to outlaw abortion effectively as the Constitution is worded currently, and therefore, they argue that the Constitution of the

United States must be amended to accommodate their particular ideology; they must revise its language if they are to cease protecting women's rights.

Alexandra DeSanctis, the ultra-conservative Catholic who provided the *New York times* with the proposed personhood amendment mentioned above in Chapter One, admits that under current conditions it may be impossible to "safeguard the equality of the unborn," and that even with the support of a right-wing Court, "states will maintain a maze of abortion laws, some of which will continue to allow abortion."[1] Thus, abortion opponents concede that a reasonable interpretation of the US Constitution can approve abortion, or at the least, accept it when a state approves it. They know that zealotry is necessary if they are to achieve their goal, which is to impose their ideology upon everyone, without exception.

The Role of Language: Its Use and Abuse[2]

It is clear that the anti-abortion movement has deliberately adopted a vocabulary, and specific language usages, that speak in absolutes in order to preclude compromise. If one concludes that abortion is murder, it is difficult if not impossible to arrive at any other than an absolutist position. That is why they insist on ridiculous definitions: not only is a fetus a "person," but so is a zygote, or a stem cell. Thus, language usage is not a simple matter of style or "correct" grammar. It is fundamental to thought and to clarity, and clarity is essential to effective communication. The speaker or writer must choose words carefully, and use them skillfully to convey the intended meaning, and *only* the intended meaning, not some other that is implied by words poorly chosen. That is why it is nec-

---

1   Alexandra DeSanctis, "The Word 'Person' Shall Apply to All Human Life—Born or Unborn," in *Seven Ideas for a 28th Amendment, Opinion, New York Times* (November 7, 2021), p. 13.

2   This section and the following section on fundamentalism/literalism are adapted from my article, "Populism and Its Perils," Annales Politologia, 22:1 (2015).

essary, even vital, to deal with language usage.

An informed public is essential to a functioning democracy. Information is required for the public to arrive at sound policy, but information alone is insufficient. To operate rationally, populations must be informed, but must also possess the skills to evaluate effectively the information that they have. As both popular literature and scholarly studies demonstrate, rational appeals do not always produce rational results. For example, the linguistic scientist George Lakoff argues that the "framing" of issues—their shaping, description, and presentation—affects an audience more powerfully than does its logic.[3]

As much as professors and intellectuals in general would like to believe that reasoned argument can persuade doubters, there is no doubt that it takes more than logic, more than reasoned argument, to be persuasive with most people. Lakoff, in other words, appears undoubtedly (and unfortunately) to be correct. Providing correct information often has little effect on opinion.

Vaccine resistance is a case in point. Regardless of the astonishing success of Covid vaccines, merely giving facts and figures will have no effect, or will result in hardening of opinion among a group that believes nonsense, such as "more people have died from the vaccines than from Covid." That such a view is preposterous, does not render it any easier to correct. Drew Westen brings social psychology to bear on the issue, and suggests similarly that rational presentations have far less success than emotional ones do.[4] This, too, is hardly disputable. Because it is so difficult to correct misinformation, it is essential to use clear and effective language to prevent misconceptions from even developing.

---

3   See George Lakoff, *Don't Think of an Elephant,* White River, Vermont: Chelsea Green Publishing, 2004; *The Political Mind,* New York: Penguin, 2009; and Lakoff and Mark Johnson, *Metaphors We Live By,* 2nd ed., Chicago: University of Chicago Press, 2003.

4   See Drew Westen, *The Political Brain,* New York: Public Affairs Press, 2008.

In order to be effective, it is essential to tailor the message to the audience, and to appeal to their emotions as well as to their intellect. The demagogue will appeal only to the emotions. An honest, intellectual, appeal can be crafted to appeal also to the emotions without sacrificing integrity. A perfect example of this may be seen in a few passages from Robert Caro's massive work on Lyndon B. Johnson. Caro can never be charged with being an LBJ partisan. His work has, in fact, been described as "demonizing" Johnson.[5] From the third volume forward, though, Caro's treatment is nuanced, thoughtful, and powerful. It presents some of the most insightful work on LBJ ever written.

Volume Four deals with LBJ's vice presidency and his early months as president. Here, Caro describes a brief speech that Vice President Johnson gave at Gettysburg Battlefield on Memorial Day weekend in 1963, a century after Lincoln's immortal Gettysburg Address there. LBJ's talk was in his own words, and he had accepted the invitation to speak on his own initiative. The Kennedy administration had shut him out entirely, and had given him no role in policy formation. The administration did not use him as an adviser (not even on civil rights), and Johnson had not submitted his speech to anyone for approval. The *Washington Post* ran his Gettysburg speech as the lead story on page one. Caro wrote that the speech had been so short, "barely two typed pages," that Johnson had read it in eight minutes. "Lincoln's speech had been short, too," Caro said, "and, the *Post* said in an editorial, this one, too, had 'eloquence . . . political courage . . . vision.'" LBJ had said, "One hundred years ago, the slave was freed . . . . One hundred years later, the Negro remains in bondage to the color of his skin. The Negro today asks justice. We do not answer him—we do not answer those who lie beneath this soil—when we reply to the Negro by asking, 'Pa-

---

5   See, e.g., Randall B. Woods, "Welcome Back to American Politics, LBJ," *History News Network*, http://hnn.us/articles/47019.html; retrieved 28 December 2021; Woods also is a biographer of LBJ (see his *Architect of American Ambition*, New York: Free Press 2006).

tience.'. . .To ask for patience from the Negro is to ask him to give more of what he has already given enough . . . . The Negro says, 'Now.' Others say, 'Never.' The voice of responsible Americans— the voices of those who died here and the great man who spoke here—their voices say, 'Together.' There is no other way."[6]

Caro described the persistence and patience with which Johnson had sought an audience alone with President Kennedy on civil rights. "May of 1963 had been the month of Birmingham." LBJ had said, "They've turned the fire hoses on a little Black girl . . . They're rolling that little girl right down the middle of the street," the month of the fierce dogs "that Bull Connor's police kept on leashes, but not tightly. And all that month, the President and the attorney general and their aides were discussing what to do in Birmingham, and whether or not to propose new civil rights legislation, and what that legislation should be, but they hadn't been discussing it with him." He kept repeating his request for a meeting with Kennedy, and met rebuff after rebuff. Finally, "at 10:00 a.m. on Monday, June 3, Johnson was allowed into the Oval Office." He was not to meet alone with the president. Already there were presidential aides Ken O'Donnell, Ted Sorensen, and the president's brother, Attorney General Robert Kennedy (RFK hated LBJ, undercutting him constantly—the hatred was mutual). "Since, at last, the President had asked Lyndon Johnson for advice about civil rights, he gave some." He did not know what was in the administration's bill, and knew of it only by reading about it in the *New York Times*, he said, nor had he sat in on any meetings, but then the master legislative strategist gave detailed advice on how to proceed—and how not to do so. His advice on strategy went unheeded.

Beyond that, this political genius LBJ who had been purely pragmatic, "who had despised politicians who talked about 'principled

---

6   Robert Caro, *The Years of Lyndon Johnson: The Passage of Power*, New York: Vintage/Random House, 2012, p. 256.

things,'" began talking about "a moral commitment." "'Negroes are tired of this patient stuff and tired of this piecemeal stuff and what they want more than anything else is not an executive order or legislation, they want a moral commitment that he's behind them.' Kennedy hadn't given them that commitment, he said. Legislation—no matter how well written it was—was only part of the answer to the civil rights problem, he said. 'The Negroes feel and they're suspicious that we're just doing what we got to do [to keep their vote].' . . . . What Negroes are really seeking is moral force and to be sure that we're on their side . . . and until they receive that assurance, unless it's stated dramatically and convincingly, they're not going to pay much attention to executive orders and legislation recommendations.' . . . And only the President himself can give them that assurance." President Kennedy then directed that LBJ and Ken O'Donnell meet to discuss the issue in more detail. They did so, and after that O'Donnell reported back to the president.

"The next morning Johnson met with Kennedy again. And that afternoon was the first of a series of meetings that had been scheduled with leaders of various groups—this one was with a hundred executives of America's largest retail chains—to mobilize opinion behind the civil rights effort. Kennedy had invited him at the last minute. And when he spoke, some members of the Kennedy Administration who had never seen Lyndon Johnson 'revved up' saw it now." The Kennedy people had notoriously derided LBJ as "Uncle Cornpone" or "Rufus Cornpone," to the delight of fellow sophisticates at their Georgetown cocktail parties and elsewhere—often within the vice president's hearing. They now had to take notice.

Presidential adviser—and certainly an intellectual force himself—Arthur Schlesinger, Jr., was present. "Schlesinger felt almost as if he were watching 'a Southern preacher.' Kennedy was 'wholly reasonable, appealing to the intellect. Johnson was evangelical. He was eloquent, all-out emotionally.' Whatever doubts Schlesinger had entertained about his sincerity on the issue evaporated that afternoon. He realized now, he was to say, that Johnson was a 'true believer.' And anyone who observed the courtesy with which the President treated him at these meetings might have imagined for a moment that Lyndon Johnson was being given, at last, a significant role in the administration." Kennedy "began to invoke him as an authority." LBJ advised Kennedy to "make the point that while he could order Negroes into a foxhole in a foreign country to fight for the American flag, he couldn't get them into southern restaurants while they were on their way to join their units to go to the war. They couldn't get a cup of coffee while they were on their way to die for the flag, he said, and with his huge hand he grabbed the flagpole of the American flag that stood beside his desk, and shook it in his rage at the injustice."[7]

This is the way in which advocates of decency and human rights need to present their arguments. Whether speaking on voter suppression, climate change, or in defense of women's reproductive rights to be free from slavery, they of course must retain their intellectual integrity and appeal to reason, but they must also craft their messages to appeal the feelings and emotions of those who might still be open to persuasion.

LBJ does not receive the credit he deserves as a powerful speaker, but at his best, he was unexcelled. His moral force comes through clearly in Caro's description, and equally strong is his intellectual force. I was not there days later as the violence occurred, but the atmosphere in Selma, Alabama the week before George Wallace's police—officially sanctioned thugs—shed the blood and broke the skulls of the civil rights demonstrators, turning them away from the Edmund Pettus bridge, as they were trying to march to Montgomery, was full of hope, excitement, tension, and fear. No one knew what was to happen.

The week after the carnage, President Lyndon Johnson on the 15th

---

7   *Ibid.*, pp. 257-262.

of March 1965 spoke to a joint session of Congress urging passage of what was to become the Voting Rights Act of 1965. Listening to the speech, watching on a black and white television in Washington, DC, however critical I may have been, I found it intellectually compelling. However cynical I may have been, I found it incredibly inspirational. As he concluded one of the most effective political speeches in the country's history, LBJ's face gradually filled the screen, and he spoke to all Americans, but especially to America's Black citizens—and he was speaking as the President of the United States. He spoke words that probably no president had ever spoken before in public, and they became his promise: "We Shall Overcome."

I literally felt chills down my spine. For a president to speak such words was enormously symbolic.

This is made all the more urgent, and all the more ironic, now that the Supreme Court, in its wisdom, decided in 2013 to emasculate LBJ's great Voting Rights Act of 1965 that had so benefited suppressed populations. No longer would Section 5 require pre-clearance in jurisdictions with a history of discrimination. With judicial straight faces the Court declared that times had changed—the infamous *Shelby County* v, *Holder* decision—that discrimination no longer existed. Much like a thoughtless patient who ceases taking the prescribed antibiotic as soon as it seems the infection is over, causing the infection to rebound, renewed by antibiotic resistance, Republicans rushed to re-implement voter suppression—on steroids, as it were.

We need assurances such as LBJ's today from all quarters to the women of the country, to the Black people of the country, to the country's Native Americans, and Brown people, to the poorest of the poor regardless of their color, as well as to other suppressed populations. We need renewed action. We need assurances such as LBJ's to the country's voters. We need powerful speakers promising the people to govern for them, not for the special interests, the bigots, the racists, the haters, the misogynists, or the greedy. The times again are filled with potential, though nothing is assured. President Biden's January speech on voting rights and against the filibuster—the speech that so offended Senator McConnell (he of stolen Supreme Court seat fame)—came closer to LBJ's than any presidential message since.

In the case of abortion, it is too late to prevent misconceptions. The anti-abortion true believers are similar to the MAGA true believers who in spite of mountains of evidence to the contrary, and no evidence at all to support their delusions, are firmly persuaded by Trumpian lies that President Biden stole the election and is not "really" president. Nevertheless, their opinions should be countered, and not permitted to stand.

Repetition of correct information, if continued for lengthy periods, may make inroads into the erroneous opinions that exist. At the least, careful language usage may prevent additional misconceptions from developing. It is important, however, and it bears repeating, that to be effective we must choose accurate words, but words that appeal emotionally, as well as intellectually.

Rarely does language receive the attention it deserves, despite the quip that the pen is mightier than the sword. When it is "weaponized," it takes on specific characteristics, and if it goes to the dark side becomes propaganda.

Propaganda—

Any study of abortion policy and its formulation should pay careful attention to public opinion. More narrowly, but possibly even more important, it should scrutinize the nature of propaganda, its uses by anti-abortionists, and their successes in shaping the discourse.

Studies of public opinion go back at least to the early 1920s, when a prominent journalist, Walter Lippmann, brought out his pioneering *Public Opinion,* a study of social psychology, media, and the ways in which attitudes develop.[8] Shortly thereafter, another journalist, Edward Bernays, an Austrian immigrant, wrote his controversial work, *Propaganda.*[9]

Bernays, a nephew of Sigmund Freud, called for the "engineering of consent," the deliberate manipulation of public opinion on behalf of both government and corporate interests using scientifically valid psychological techniques. He saw propaganda as a social good (though he used it to benefit commercial interests, including the American Tobacco Company, hardly devoted to the public good). One should note that the term "propaganda" at the time had little of the negative connotation that emerged so forcefully in the 1930s, when Stalin's Soviet Union on the left, and various Fascist dictatorships on the right—especially Germany under Hitler's misnamed "National Socialism"—used scientific techniques to warp language and shape public opinion. Manipulation, distortion, and abuse of language led to violence and terror.

The roots, though, reach further back than formal studies. Both Lippmann and Bernays had been key officials during World War One of President Woodrow Wilson's "Committee on Public Information," headed by George Creel; the notorious "Creel Committee." The blurb on the 2005 edition credits Bernays with "eerily prescient vision for regimenting the collective mind," and suggests that his *Propaganda* is "an essential read for all who wish to understand how power is used by the ruling elite of our society."

Propaganda has advanced by orders of magnitude since Bernays, but he set the tone for much advertising in the 1930s and subsequently. Understanding modern propaganda helps to understand

---

8   Walter Lippmann, *Public Opinion,* New York: Harcourt Brace, 1922.

9   Edward Bernays, *Propaganda,* New York: H. Liveright, 1928.

the forces that have shaped anti-abortion legislation, and also provides insights into public discourse on the subject. Much of the approach employed by anti-abortionists seems to have adopted techniques the United States employed during the Cold War to differentiate the "American Way of Life" from that of "Godless Communism." Wendy Wall has analyzed brilliantly the use of propaganda techniques directed toward "Inventing the 'American Way.'"[10] The Advertising Council, the National Association of Manufacturers, and corporate interests in general were concerned with friction between management and labor, and sought national unity during World War II and thereafter. They portrayed a "tripod of freedom," that did incorporate such praiseworthy goals as civil liberties, representative democracy, religious freedom, and opposition to racism while concentrating on political goals such as anticommunism and, above all, "economic freedom."

To do so they drank deeply from the well of American popular culture and in the 1940s and 1950s conscripted even Superman, who became their spokesman for "Truth, Justice, and the American Way," as they attempted to roll back the reforms of the New Deal. This campaign by the business community did not achieve all its goals, but on some levels it was so successful that that many Americans and some of their more noisy political leaders now seem to think of the term "free enterprise" as having been a prime factor in the American Revolution, perhaps a key principle of the Constitution, and possibly even having been conferred upon the nation by Christianity itself (or, among the more ecumenical, by the "Judeo-Christian tradition"). Wall, though, demonstrates that the term hardly existed before 1935 when "America's corporate leaders" adopted a specific political strategy.[11]

After World War Two and Nazi Germany's downfall, the noted liter-

---

10   Wendy Wall, *Inventing the "American Way,"* New York: Oxford University Press, 2008.

11   *Ibid.,* pp. 48-49.

ary and cultural critic George Steiner, wrote of the corruption of the German language. The Nazis gleefully manufactured unparalleled linguistic ugliness and imposed it for their own sadistic purposes. They created mass barbarism and delusion among intelligent, and even educated, people—actually controlling a population.

Steiner argued that languages can demonstrate that they have within themselves the germs of their own dissolution. "Actions of the mind that were once spontaneous become mechanical, frozen habits (dead metaphors, stock similes, slogans). Words grow longer and more ambiguous. Instead of style, there is rhetoric. Instead of precise common usage, there is jargon."[12] To be sure, Steiner admits, a Hitler would have found "venom and moral illiteracy" in any language, but German was "ready to give hell a native tongue." He asked how could a word such as *spritzen* "recover a sane meaning after having signified to millions the spurting of Jewish blood from knife points?"[13] Words, he said, gradually lost their meanings "and acquired nightmarish definitions. *Jude, Pole, Russe* came to mean two-legged lice, putrid vermin which good Aryans must squash, as a party manual said, 'like roaches on a dirty wall.' 'Final solution,' *endgültige Lösung,* came to signify the death of six million human beings in gas ovens." Beyond the bestialities, the language was called upon "to enforce numerous falsehoods," to say "light" when there was darkness, "victory," when there was defeat."[14] This happened to a language, even though it is language "that has been the vessel of human grace and the prime carrier of civilization."[15]

---

12   George Steiner, "The Hollow Miracle," from Max J. Skidmore, ed., *Word Politics: Essays on Language and Politics,* Palo Alto, CA: Freel and Associates, pp. 25-38 (page numbers are from this volume); reprinted with permission of Atheneum from George Steiner, *Essays on Language, Literature, and the Inhuman,* New York: Atheneum, 1970; originally published in *The Reporter Magazine* (18 February 1960). Quotation, pp.27-28.

13   *Ibid.,* p. 29.

14   *Ibid.,* p. 30.

15   *Ibid.,* p. 38.

Fortunately, the German language demonstrated resilience, and did recover.

German was not unique, except possibly in the extremes to which it went. George Orwell has pointed to similar, if less dramatic, tendencies in English,[16] and modern political discourse in America and elsewhere is hardly reassuring.

Nor is it reassuring to note the anomaly that America gave to the world the principles of the Declaration of Independence—life, liberty, the pursuit of happiness, political equality, and self government—yet in America there recently have been chants of "Jews will not replace us," anti-abortionists borrow from the horrors of the Holocaust to condemn women to subordination by equating reproductive choice with mass murder, and there has been fierce resistance from white nationalists (and the more "respectable conservatives") to "1619," the project in the *New York Times* that presented the role of racism in American history. America is not, and has not been, racist, they scream, yet the Nazis—as they fastened their totalitarian claws into German culture and government—found in American racist legislation, especially from the slavery and Jim Crow periods in the south, perfect models for their own policies undergirding their Third Reich's "Final Solution" of genocide.

In the late 1930s, America was bombarded by right-wing extremist propaganda from the extreme right in Nazi Germany, and also from the extreme left in the Stalinist Soviet Union. The propaganda barrage brought sincere efforts to counter the assaults upon language. The most prominent of these was the Institute for Propaganda Analysis. The New York Public library has the Institute's records, two linear feet (two boxes), in the Manuscripts and Archives Division.[17] The Library indicates that a group of social science schol-

---

16 See George Orwell, "Politics and the English Language," originally published in the magazine *Horizon* (April 1946), but reprinted countless times (including in my *Word Politics*), and widely available.

17 Call Number: MssCol 1513 http://catalog.nyuplorg, preferred citation: "In-

ars founded the Institute in New York City in 1937 in order to en-able to enable the public to "detect and analyze propaganda." The IPA conducted research into the methods developed to influence public opinion, it published analyses of current problems, and it promoted the establishment of study groups in public schools for detecting propaganda. It published a monthly bulletin, *Propaganda Analysis* from 1937 to 1941. Additionally, the institute produced a number of books, the most prominent of which was *The Fine Art of* Propaganda, by Alfred McClung Lee and Elizabeth Briant Lee,[18] which analyzed radio speeches of the populist and anti-Semitic demagogue, Father Charles Coughlin. The IPA also produced oth-er publications, such as *Propaganda Analysis*, the *Group Leader's Guide to Propaganda Analysis, and Propaganda: How to Recognize and Deal with it.*

The New York Public Library's IPA website mentions these, and the IPA's "seven common propaganda devices, "The ABCs of Pro-paganda Analysis." These formed the basis for flyers and other ma-terials supplied to schools, colleges, and "adult civic groups," and were the best known of the IPA's works. Americans of a certain age (I include myself) are likely to remember classroom materi-als from their school days that built around these seven techniques from IPA's publication, *Propaganda Analysis*:

Name Calling—

Glittering Generalities—The propagandist uses them to create a favorable reaction to whatever is desired. A notable recent example is "family values."

Transfer—this device uses the authority and prestige of some-thing hearers respect or revere to associate it with something he or

---

stitute for Propaganda Analysis records, Manuscripts and Archives Division, The New York Public Library; note: access requires advance notification.

18   Alfred McClung Lee and Elizabeth Briant Lee, *The Fine Art of Propaganda*, New York: Harcourt Brace, 1939.

she is trying to get hearers to accept.

Testimonial—originally, this meant the obvious: associating something the propagandist wants accepted with a figure whom the hearer respects, one who was presumed to be an expert on the propagandist's subject. Now it often includes entertainers, sports figures, or other celebrities often without regard to expertise.

Plain Folks—the use of an obviously populist technique to assert humble background, implying that it is superior to one of privilege.

Card Stacking—In this technique, half-truth masquerades as truth. A mediocre candidate becomes an "intellectual titan." Extremist elements become "freedom fighters."

Bandwagon—this technique "employs symbols, colors, music, movement, and all the dramatic arts" to convince the populace that "everyone agrees" that thus and so should be done, and that anyone who disagrees is out of step.

The Institute for Propaganda Analysis had a few quite active years, but "was dormant during World War II and in 1950 all operations ceased."[19] Upon reflection, it would seem inevitable that the IPA would be controversial. Critics argued that it was too negative, that its efforts were simplistic, or that analyzing advertising would damage capitalism or the economy. An obvious objection would be that the habit of examining news for enemy propaganda would include building a resistance to America's own wartime propaganda and thus undermine national solidarity. According to the New York Public Library's materials, though, the IPA "maintains the reason it suspended its operations in 1942 was due to lack of sufficient funds and not the war."

Undoubtedly, the techniques the IPA identified remain with us today, all over the world, throughout all political parties, and from

---

19   New York Public Library Archives and Manuscripts, http://archives.nypl.
org/mss/1513 ; retrieved 28 December 2021.

candidates on all points along the political spectrum. They have, of course, been revised and expanded.

The Threat from Fundamentalism and Literalism—

There is yet another force that may be potentially even more important than propaganda techniques. It certainly is related to language but is a force that works overtly against language itself, and even the foundation of much of rational thought, logic.

Earlier, I criticized fundamentalism, and disregarding technical definitions, I defined it as literalism. Especially in the United States, there is a strong movement that emerged from fundamentalist religion, but which has strongly influenced politics, economics, and other realms of human endeavor. It appears to be creating vast numbers of voters—and officeholders as well—who are mentally armed against science, against logical argument, and against the very elements of rational thought.

It is called "harmonization," and springs from the need to protect the idea of biblical inerrancy; the belief that every word in the Bible is literally true. There are numerous inconsistencies in scripture, and instances of clear contradiction as well. The technique at work is easy to overlook or to dismiss, but a cultural anthropologist, Susan Friend Harding, examined it in a remarkable study, *The Book of Jerry Falwell: Fundamentalist Language and Politics*.[20] She describes the process at length. As I put it in a review, "To the outsider, the most startling and ominous of Harding's findings is the manner in which—in a defiance of reason—contradiction actually strengthens faith. The Bible is literally true in every respect. Identifying inconsistencies simply tests faith and (postmodernists take note) forces an acceptance of the inconsistent whole." Believers are forced to harmonize "contradictions and infelicities according to interpretive conventions that presume, and thus reveal, God's design." In this

---

20   Susan Friend Harding, *The Book of Jerry Falwell: Fundamentalist Language and Politics*, Princeton: Princeton University Press, 2000.

sense adherents of biblical literalism are "largely—if not completely—shielded against any challenge to their belief; shielded against inroads from the very bases of modern thought: logic and reason."[21]

Many Bible colleges that train fundamentalist ministers have specific courses in "harmonization," courses that deal with biblical inconsistencies and contradictions. The courses indoctrinate until students can accept impossible propositions as true, eliminating awareness that if one thing is true, the other cannot be. This does not mean that fundamentalists are unaware of biblical inconsistencies—they tend to be too well versed in scripture to argue that. Vincent Crapanzano, also an anthropologist, immersed himself in the world of fundamentalism, as did Harding. He says that most of the fundamentalists he interviewed are not bothered by biblical inconsistencies, and often ignore them. "There simply was one meaning, God's meaning—the plain, ordinary meaning, and one intention, God's intention, that was manifested through the divinely inspired authors of Scripture." Fundamentalists, he argues, "adhere to what is popularly called a 'domino approach' to the Bible. For them to admit even one error in Scripture would be to destroy their faith in the whole." This, he says, illustrates the "all-or-nothing" quality of fundamentalism.[22] When asked about biblical contradictions, many he interviewed dismissed them by saying such things "only appear as contradictions because we cannot understand God's words fully."[23]

The argument here is not to attack the doctrine of biblical inerrancy, or any theological principle, nor to judge what is appropriate for a religion; it is absolutely to say that such thought is dangerous out-

---

21   Max J. Skidmore, "Review of Susan Friend Harding, *The Book of Jerry Falwell*," from *The European Legacy* 7:3 (July 2002), 415-416; reprinted in Joey Skidmore, *The Review as Art and Communication*, London: Cambridge Scholars Publishing, 2013, 87-89.

22   Vincent Crapanzano, *Serving the Word: Literalism in America from the Pulpit to the Bench*, New York: The New press, 2000, pp. 60-63.

23   *Ibid.*, p. 79.

side the theological realm. If large numbers of people are trained to dismiss logical contradiction within their religion as though it is unimportant, they may think similarly when dealing with abortion, economics, politics, or other phenomena in the secular world. This is especially true in the United States, in which the power of fundamentalists has become a major force in one of its two major political parties. Alternatively, they may believe they are thinking logically, and looking at all the facts when in fact they are ignoring arguments that contradict their own. This is painfully obvious when anti-abortionists set forth their litany of reasons to oppose abortion, while simultaneously ignoring even the existence—let alone the rights—of the pregnant woman. In other words, they assign an entire realm of "rights" to a fetus, even an embryo, and ignore or totally reject the rights of a complete and fully functioning human being, the potential mother.

Is it unreasonable to think that fundamentalist religion's dismissal of evolution, for example, may be related outside of churches to rejection of scientific arguments, such as the reality of human-induced warming of the planet, or the safety, or the efficacy of vaccines for Covid 19? Brendan Nyhan, who teaches government at Dartmouth College, published an op ed piece in the *New York Times* that may be relevant here. He pointed to a study by Yale Law School professor, Dan Kahan, demonstrating that those who dismiss evolution and human-influenced climate change may be well informed, "they knew the science; they just weren't willing to say that they believed in it." In other words, if scientific consensus "contradicts their political or religious views," they refuse to let that consensus affect their opinion. Nyhan says that his own research and that of his colleagues supports Kahan's findings, and that "Factual and scientific evidence is often ineffective at reducing misperceptions and can even backfire on issues like weapons of mass destruction, health care reform and vaccines. With science, as with politics, identity often trumps the facts."

The next day, economist Paul Krugman in his own column cited Nyhan's essay and demonstrated that the same phenomenon affects many of even the most distinguished professional economists—especially with regard to monetary matters. Issues that should be strictly factual and based entirely on evidence, instead were overridden by "faith." The problem was not ignorance, it was wishful thinking, he concluded. The economic disaster of 2008 was caused by a housing bubble, but mainstream economists (while initially shocked at the developments) "quickly rallied." Somehow, they concluded that the financial crisis had been the "fault of liberals." The great danger then facing the economy came, not from the crisis itself, "but from the efforts of policy makers to limit the damage." Both economists and politicians such as Paul Ryan began to issue "dire warnings," about "printing money," warning "currency debasement and inflation" would ensue. That this did not happen in no way affected their arguments. Krugman noted that it is hardly the first time that "a politically appealing economic doctrine has been proved wrong by events," but that most of the analysts have followed the same flawed approach of climate-change deniers. They "have gone down the conspiracy-theory rabbit hole," and claim that, despite the evidence, "we really do have soaring inflation, but the government is lying about the numbers." Note this was in 2014.

He asked why monetary theory is being treated like evolution or climate-change, rather than simply responding to the numbers, and concludes that "money is indeed a kind of theological issue." Precisely in line with the argument of this article, Krugman says that "when faith—including faith-based economics—meets evidence, evidence doesn't have a chance."[24]

Crapanzano does not allege that literalism in the law is rooted in American evangelicalism. He does not look to their religion to dis-

---

24   Paul Krugman, "Belief, Facts And Money," *The New York Times* (7 July 2014), A17.

cern the roots of the interpretations of the legal literalists. "My aim is to delineate a mode of interpretation, whatever its source," he says.[25]

This, I agree, is what is important. Nevertheless, I argue that it would be unwise not to recognize the potential effect of fundamentalist thought—and literalist thought in general—on policy. Because of America's overwhelming world influence, for example, fundamentalist thought on American policy is almost always pernicious. In years past the US has banned "needle-exchange programs (thus contributing to the spread of AIDS), and family-planning programs, (thus contributing to poverty, starvation, and the subjugation of women)."[26] Moreover, religious extremism has effects even beyond US policy. Uganda's 2014 Anti-Homosexuality Law provides life sentences for homosexuals. Uganda had laws against homosexuality as legacies of British colonialism, but the impetus for the recent cruelty came from American evangelists, active in Uganda conducting seminars, speaking publicly, and working closely with government officials there.

Undoubtedly there are many who are aware of the dangers, but there are too few. Policies around the world reflect the influence of right-wing extremists, white nationalists, and those wrapped up and packaged by the all-purpose epithet: wingnuts. If they have the ability to exercise influence abroad, it would be the height of foolishness to ignore the effect that they might have here at home. It does not take a very careful look to recognize that such an effect is already here. It is fortunately that the former president was not more capable, but his legacy and continuing influence is causing untold harm to American institutions that are far more fragile than anyone recognized. We are on the threshold of an American fascism, and there needs to be widespread recognition that it needs to be crushed, or it will crush the rest of us.

---

25 Crapanzano, *Serving the Word*, xviii.

26 Max J. Skidmore, "Review," 89.

CHAPTER FIVE

ABORTION RESTRICTIONS AND UNLIMITED GOVERNMENT

Most governments dominated by the far right tend to have roots in religion. They tend to use religion to secure obedience and maintain social control. It requires no special attention to recognize that anti-abortion policies are common in such regimes, whether religious or secular, nor to recognize that far-right modes of thought lend themselves to becoming obsessions (far left modes of thought do as well, but contrary to the fantasies on the right, ultra-left ideologies have never been serious competitors for power in the US). Campaigns against abortion are one of the most useful tactics of dictators of the right.

Although certainly not limited to rightest regimes—the term in fact arose to describe a leftist totalitarianism, Stalinism—the tendency to develop cults of personality also is especially persistent. Consider the cult of Reagan idealization among Republicans that lasted some quarter of a century after his presidency. The numerous debates in 2008 among Republican candidates seeking the presidential nomination saw an almost worshipful—and pathetic—effort of every candidate to claim forcefully to be the "most like Ronald Reagan."

Consider, also, how the obsession with Reagan became, almost overnight, an even more hysterical commitment to Donald Trump after he burst onto the scene, stumbled into the presidency, engineered a chaotic, cruel, and irrational administration, only to lose his re-election bid decisively in 2020. Then, on inauguration day in January 2021, he was defenestrated after his unexpected and deplorable assumption of the presidency four years previously. In view of his whining, fantasizing about actually having won, and demonstrating that he is a monumentally sore loser he left office with even more ill grace than when he assumed it. Surely history will remember him as America's—possibly as the world's—worst loser of all time. Certainly, with his inciting a near guerrilla warfare by his deluded followers, he is the most dangerous loser ever. Possibly the only thing that would have been more dangerous would have been for him to have won.

Trump's election victory in 2016 was hardly impressive politically. He was a popular-vote loser. His win was a fluke because of the unfortunate nature of the electoral college. His subsequent effort in 2020 to secure re-election led to electoral disaster for Republicans at the national level. That time he lost the popular vote by more than 7 million—as opposed to his roughly 3 million loss in 2016—and was trounced in the all-important electoral college. All the while, his Republicans were losing both houses of Congress, each of which ultimately went to the Democrats.

Regardless, the Republicans' Trump obsession, if anything, intensified. The party over the years had become adept at ignoring truth and fact. One should recall the Republican official in the Bush administration who suggested that the "reality-based community" didn't exist, and that Republicans created their own reality. After Trump, the denial of reality had become complete. As a party, Republicans had lost the ability even to recognize truth or fact. They had, in fact, come to assume that truth or fact consisted only in what their losing candidate or his most fervent henchmen proclaimed, such as the enormous lie that the election had been "rigged." Recent studies indicate that only a small fraction of Trump voters believe that Biden had won the election fairly. Failure may not be an option, but it hardly makes a dent in Republican worship for cult figures.

Anti-abortion commitments, similarly, become obsessions. They are among the most likely to be dominant among the ideas of political True Believers, in the Eric Hoffer sense. Hoffer wrote in 1951 of the delusions of mass movements, and gave recognition to language that inspired resentment and anger, and that generate activists that provided the energy and organization. His classic work remains available.[1]

In fact, of all far-right policies that lend themselves to becoming obsessions, those opposing abortion are among the most forceful. That was why Frank Schaeffer's politicization of American fundamentalist/evangelicals was so successful. He created an anti-abortion mania among previously uninterested Protestants, even enabling the strongly-anti-Catholic right to bridge their differences with the Church, and to enter into alliance with their former arch enemies, whom they considered not really to be Christian (at least until it became politically expedient to change their opinion).

Perhaps less astonishing, fundamentalist/evangelical Protestants became arguably the single major force in the Republican Party. The "religionized" GOP then—again, more astonishing—admitted into their cabal a Mormon. Fundamentalist/evangelicals had been, if anything, even more opposed to Mormons than to Catholics. Nevertheless, they and their Republican Party threw their support behind a Mormon, Mitt Romney, who became their presidential candidate in 2012, running with a Catholic candidate for vice president, no less. Obviously, the Republican label meant more to them than theology did. Strange bedfellows.

There are connections here that may be camouflaged, and unrecognized, but that should be troubling. Anti-abortion policies encourage conservative, even far-right, policies. This does not mean—and I am not saying—that all who oppose abortion are right-wing extremists, nor does it mean that all American conservatives are sympathetic to violence or white nationalism, nor that all Republicans

---

1 Eric Hoffer, *The True Believer: Thoughts on the Nature of Mass Movements*, Harper and Row, 1951.

are extremists. What it does mean is that all these groups, some no doubt unknowingly, share common elements; they are singing from the same hymn book, as it were.

American mainstream "conservatism," as I made clear previously, is not as far from the most irrational and violent elements in American politics as it might seem.[2] There is a close association between "respectable, mainstream, American conservatism," and the violent extremist right, members of which often live in the woods, withdraw from society, and practice for insurrection.

During the Obama administration, it became plain that threats against a Black president, and to the established order, were building. Government agents began investigating, causing Republican officials to explode in outrage at what they called investigations into "conservatives." As a matter of fact, they had a point. Intuitively, they recognized that investigations into right-wing extremists would almost assuredly expose connections with "ordinary conservatives."

The Obama administration, responding to the criticisms, backed down and ceased its investigations, leaving police officials handicapped later when white nationalist atrocities began to intensify. Such violent groups and their atrocities had always existed, but because they had tended to be directed toward Black Americans and their communities, the white mainstream generally was ignorant of them, or at least considered them to be unimportant. Having taken over the Republican Party to a large extent, the white nationalist extremists now have expanded their targets to include all outside their cultish ranks; even to the extent of undermining the very principle of popular government.

People around the globe watched in fascinated horror the spectacle of a full-fledged, if inept, coup attempt on January 6, 2021, following exhortations from a sitting president, Donald Trump, to

---

2   See *Common Sense Manifesto*, p. 42

come to Washington and be "wild;" also, to "fight like hell." They did, seeking to undo the election that clearly had rebuffed Trump and chosen Joe Biden. Since then, investigations and prosecutions of those involved have continued.

Defending popular government requires recognition of its complexity. Regardless of flaws in execution, the principles of the Declaration of Independence and the Constitution are designed to defend both popular rule, and individual liberties. These may come into conflict, making it essential to recognize that each is important, each must be defended, and that at times, defending them requires nuance. The task therefore is not simple; there is truth to the trite saying (that often is used to mean its opposite), "Freedom isn't free." To be sure; it also can mean defending what one dislikes.

Here we come to a key issue regarding abortion, an issue that is vital, but astonishingly, is almost completely ignored by supporters of reproductive rights, while completely unrecognized by opponents. Most of those opposing abortion seem also to profess to be in favor of limited government and of human freedom. Conservatives, including anti-abortionists, tend to rage against "government power," and especially against "unelected government bureaucrats."

An effective anti-abortion policy, though, a policy that actually seeks to eliminate abortion and not merely to give lip service to those who call themselves "pro-life," *requires* a powerful government; possibly even a totalitarian one. Part of that government would be "empowered bureaucrats."

An effective abortion policy would immediately place every human female who becomes pregnant, women or girls, under the control of government officials. Pregnancy would immediately empower the government, to strip from women all control over their own bodies. Anti-abortion policies also have implications for those fertile females who are not pregnant; in order to be truly effective at eliminating abortions, all people capable of becoming pregnant would have to be subject to periodic examinations to ensure that they were not pregnant, and to inform the government if they were.

This without a doubt reflects duplicity common among conservatives. When they say they oppose government power, their underlying is phrased cautiously to avoid being alarming, but what they mean is generally that they oppose the exercise of power to assist ordinary people. They oppose power used to keep people from having to fend for themselves, giving them some protection from the forces arrayed against them. Conservatives are likely to favor power used to *make* people fend for themselves.

When it comes to the true coercive power of government—police and military power; that is, the power to protect property and propertied interests from domestic and foreign interference—American conservatives tend to favor boosting the power of government to regulate conduct, and to control the actions of people who might intrude upon elite interests. Elite interests equal conservative interests. Making voting as difficult as possible for those likely to vote against them is an illustration of how their intentions are skewed to favor elites. Conservatives, when their own interests require it, are quite willing to violate the liberty of the general public. They fail to recognize that, in the long run, that exercise of power can be turned back upon themselves.

Abortion's opponents overlook an inconvenient fact regarding government power. When they empower government to usurp women's rights, they are empowering government with the ability to strip rights from others as well; from *anyone* else; even from themselves.

Power granted to oppress others can be turned against them. Certainly, the government that has the power to prevent abortions, under a different kind of authoritarian rule would have the power to *require* abortions. That other side of the coin is not an imaginative figment. Consider the case of China. Similarly, on the other end of the continuum, the extreme right. Hitler's Nazis used abortion both ways: they forbade it for "Aryan" women, and under many circumstances required it for others.

If a government can forbid abortions, that means, of course, that it can require a pregnant woman to give birth. Would it be much different for a government to require fertile females to *become* pregnant?

President Franklin D. Roosevelt brilliantly described the proper uses of government, and the improper uses. Properly used, government is to serve the people; improperly used, it enslaves them. In 1941, FDR formulated and described his "Four Freedoms," incorporating both continuity, and subtle change. "'Freedom' has always been a cardinal tenet of the American ideology, and when the President proclaimed the 'freedom of speech' and 'freedom of religion' he was thoroughly in accord with American tradition. But when he went on to speak of 'freedom from want,' and 'freedom from fear,' he was, in a sense, departing from that tradition—or, rather, enlarging upon it. He added two parts security under the label of 'freedom.'"[3]

It was "freedom" that FDR expanded appropriately, making it more relevant to the people. Elsewhere, he snatched the word and the notion away from its abusers, so that it would *continue* to benefit the people, and not be used to trick them into slavery. Adding to the Bill of Rights, in his state of the union address in 1944 he called for a Second (or an Economic) Bill of Rights.[4] He echoed that call again in his final such address in 1945. In ringing language that always causes American conservatives to cringe at the very

---

3   Max J. Skidmore, *Medicare and the American Rhetoric of Reconciliation*, Tuscaloosa: University of Alabama Press, 1970; reprinted Questia Media, 2000; p. 4.

4   See Cass Sunstein's brilliant study of FDR's proposal: *The Second Bill of Rights: FDR's Unfinished Revolution and Why We Need It More Than Ever*, New York: Basic Books, 2004.

thought of enhanced rights for the people, FDR called for implementation of:

The right to a useful and remunerative job in the industries or shops or farms or mines of the nation;

The right to earn enough to provide adequate food and clothing and recreation;

The right of every farmer to raise and sell his products at a return which will give him and his family a decent living;

The right of every businessman, large and small, to trade in an atmosphere of freedom from unfair competition and domination by monopolies at home or abroad;

The right of every family to a decent home;

The right to adequate medical care and the opportunity to achieve and enjoy good health;

The right to adequate protection from the economic fears of old age, sickness, accident, and unemployment'

The right to a good education.

With the addition of protections for the environment, and some revisions in language to recognize sexual equality, this is a sound, sober, and—yes—informed common sense approach to American rights. Yet, after some three quarters of a century, it remains unachieved, and continues to be perceived as "radical."

Consider our language usage: today, journalists, often even "liberal" journalists, who want to discuss "radical" ideas that are too far left in the Democratic Party to be practical, tend invariably to condense them to "Medicare for all," and "the Green New Deal." Yet these are hardly radical, they are nothing more than common-sense. Every other advanced industrial country provides full health care for their entire populations, with no large costs to any individual. Why is any proposal to do the same, regardless of the mechanism, considered extreme in the United States? The effects of a warming planet responding to human activities are almost universally recognized as an existential concern, possibly threatening life itself, and certainly threatening civilization as we know it. Why are proposals to protect the environment in a manner to strengthen the economy, and simultaneously to make life better, not simply recognized as common sense, instead of as dangerous? Efforts to protect business profits in the short run certainly cannot be justified under any logic if they result in a destruction of the entire systems human beings have constructed. If the planet is destroyed business, and profits, go to hell along with everything else.

So, what does "freedom," or "liberty" mean? FDR not only struck fear into the hearts of those he called 'economic royalists,' he expanded the notion of freedom to protect, not suppress, the people. Freedom does not mean—and cannot be permitted to mean— freedom for the wealthy to control the lives of others. Liberty does not mean—and cannot be permitted to mean—liberty, for a business to impose its religion on its employees.

FDR said "that he did not favor a 'return to that definition of liberty under which for many years a free people were being gradually regimented into the service of the privileged few.'"[5] Going beyond FDR but consistent with his expanded view of liberty or freedom, his addition of rights, liberty and freedom do not mean—and cannot be permitted to mean—the "right" of a zygote, an embryo, or a fetus to cancel every right of a whole, fully functioning human being, and regiment her, enslave her, under the dictates of an all-powerful government. In other words, they cannot be interpreted to mean outlawing abortion, without infringing upon basic human rights.

---

5   Quoted in Max J. Skidmore, "Review of Wendy L. Wall, *Inventing the American Way: The Politics of Consensus From the New Deal to the Civil Rights Movement,* Chapel Hill: Oxford University Press, 2008," in *Journal of American Culture,* 34:4 (December 2011), pp. 414-415.

These are considerations that surely should give sincere opponents of abortion, those who genuinely oppose it for religious or philosophical reasons, cause to hesitate. American "conservatives" as a rule, though, would likely be unpersuaded; they continually seek to preserve the power arrangements that keep themselves in control. They favor controls on power only when others exercise the power; that is, when power's exercise compromises their interests.

A government that is restrictive regarding women's reproduction will be a government that is restrictive in other ways, as well, often in most other ways. Some may dispute this. America, they say, is the "land of the brave and the home of the free," yet abortion was forbidden Until *Roe* v. *Wade*, (that is, until the *Roe* decision in 1973). Abortion restrictions did not go hand in hand with repressive government, they insist.

That argument would bring scorn from much of the Native American Indian population. That population has been subjugated, its members systematically have been robbed of their land, there is today a notorious and largely uninvestigated disappearance of Native women from reservations (certainly kidnapped and murdered), and government policies historically have sought to destroy Native American Indian culture. Currently, it seems unsafe to live as a woman on a reservation.

In March of 2021, the House overwhelmingly passed a bill reauthorizing the Violence Against Women Act. The vote included substantial Republican support. Among many provisions improving this already excellent act, it has expanded provisions intended to protect Native women. At this writing, January of 2022, Senate Republicans continue to block the bill. That should speak for itself in enlightening any woman considering how she should vote—and in a just world, any man as well. For additional considerations in this regard, please refer to chapter seven on personal protection.

Similarly, ask of America's Black population how many of them, es-

pecially Black men, have been abused, even executed by police officers, because they committed the crime of "driving while Black," or,
more broadly, the simple act of failing to show adequate deference
to, or respect for, the officer. Sometimes there was no reason at all,
merely an officer's nervous reaction to a non-threatening gesture,
or worse. Think of the number of Black citizens murdered by police
because of "changing lanes without signaling," driving with something dangling from a rearview mirror, or having a burned-out tail-
light. How many white citizens have even been stopped because of
these made-up excuses, or killed because they were unarmed, but
"using their cars as a weapon"? How many Black women have been
arrested who had committed no crime other than minor traffic violations, who then were found dead in their jail cells?

How many Black women—or white women as well—receive
substandard care in or out of hospitals, because their complaints
were ignored? How many women have been placed in "conserva-
torships" when men in the same circumstances almost assuredly
would not have been? How many people in general, but women
and children in particular, have been abused by immigration officials as a result of the draconian policies developed by former attorney general Jeff Sessions and enthusiastically implemented by the
disgraced former president?

How many Black Americans since the end of Reconstruction were
expelled from so-called "Sundown Towns" that forbade them to be
within the town limits after dark? James Loewen studied the subject intensively, and identified hundreds of such towns all across
the country with the notable, and ironic, exception of the south.
Southern Whites were never uncomfortable with the presence of
Black Americans, so long as they were subordinate. Southern institutions, in fact, having been built on slavery, required them to be
present to serve the Whites.

Across the country there were lynchings, both north and south.
Outside the south, they served to keep Black people out of sight,

out of mind, and out. Loewen demonstrates that although the sundown signs may be gone, their legacy persists, with that legacy being fully White suburbs and other fully White areas.[6] Those of us of a certain age may remember the signs, particularly in the Midwest, the West, and the Ozarks.

The culture, itself, was oppressive of women. Brewers and distillers financed the post-Civil War "saloon," that enticed low-paid workers, served them free, salty, food to increase thirst. "The result was too often disastrous for families, with extensive abuse of women for whom neither law nor society offered protection."[7] The result of the pressure for reform was extreme and disastrous, and led to the beginnings of organized crime in this country: prohibition. Although Wyoming entered the Union in 1890 with the vote for women, and a number of states in the next few years had granted women the vote, there was no national guarantee that women could vote until ratification of the Nineteenth Amendment in 1920. Rights, though, came slowly. As late as 1970 it was difficult, if not impossible, for a woman to have a credit card, secure a mortgage, or otherwise obtain financing without a husband's signature; or, for unmarried women, their father's or brother's!

How many American citizens even now, in the 21st century, have been abused by officials under auspices of the Patriot Act? How many beginning in the late 20th century by governmental power generated by the War on Drugs? Largely because of America's drug policies since the Nixon administration, and eagerly accelerated by Reagan's, federal prison capacity has increased at a rate far greater than the population increase. Reported figures vary, but it is reasonable to say that it increased by as much as five times.

---

6   James W. Loewen, *Sundown Towns: A Hidden Dimension of American Racism*, New York: Touchstone Books, 2005.

7   Max J. Skidmore, "Review of Daniel Okrent, *Last Call: The Rise and Fall of Prohibition*, New York: Scriber, 2020; in *Journal of American Culture*, 35:1 (March 20120, pp. 82-84.

CHAPTER FIVE: ABORTION RESTRICTIONS AND UNLIMITED GOVERNMENT

This is exacerbated by the odious practice common throughout the country of employing private companies to run prisons. That is, enabling businesses to convert correctional institutions into profit-making organizations, using public resources and authorities to enrich themselves and their investors. There are many troubles that this creates, including highly questionable practice of delegating public powers, police powers, to private organizations to permit them to use public authority for private gain.

Going back more than a century and a half, this was the principle that so enraged Andrew Jackson and his supporters, leading them to attack the Bank of the United States. As bad as private profit from public money, profiting from crime and misery is far more questionable. When he left office, President Eisenhower in 1961 warned in his great farewell address of a "military-industrial complex" that was warping and corrupting American politics. We now have a parallel, often identified as a "prison-industrial complex," that is similarly corrupting.

The dynamic of this prison-industrial complex is obviously to economize, to hold expenditures to a minimum to achieve maximum return on investment, leading to deprivation within the institutions, and certainly not "correction." Mistreatment of prisoners also creates seething resentments and mental troubles, ultimately causing definite dangers to the public. The tendency among conservatives is to adopt a "lock 'em up and throw away the key" mentality that at best removes much of their motivation for reform. Privatized prisons lead to powerful lobbying of legislatures to continue harsh sentencing policies.

It is significant, and not in a good way, that despite the enormous size of some other countries—a number of them such as China, notoriously police states—the United States incarcerates far more of its population than any other nation. That is hardly the mark of a "free society," but our own population, that is, our white population, hardly notices; at least until they are affected.

This is not alarmist. There can be no doubt regarding the totalitarian nature of policies directed at women that actually do exist, in contemporary America. These policies exist because of the obsession of the far right to eliminate abortion.

Michelle Goldberg, writing in the *New York Times* on the 19th of October 2021, describes additional outrages. Her column's title is apt: "When a Miscarriage is Manslaughter."

A young woman in Oklahoma, Brittney Poolaw, 19 years old, was arrested last year after suffering a miscarriage. Unable to afford a $20,000 bond, she was jailed for a year and a half awaiting trial. When the trial took place, it lasted one day. Poolaw had had no medical care. She had not attempted an abortion. Even though she admitted having used "both methamphetamine and marijuana," the prosecution's own expert witness could not say that her drug use had caused her to miscarry.

Nevertheless, a venomous prosecutor, who no doubt sought to add to a list of convictions, persuaded a gullible and malleable jury to convict. Ms Poolaw received a sentence of four years in prison. This bears repetition: a young woman received a prison sentence because she suffered a miscarriage, a naturally occurring phenomenon. This took place not under Hitler or Stalin—actually, and with the height of irony, as evil as they were, it probably would not have taken place under Hitler or Stalin—but in the United States of America, a country that ostensibly is devoted to individual rights. Despite the Declaration of Independence and the Constitution, the "understandings" of anti-abortion ideologues (for example, that "personhood" occurs at the instant of conception) now at times are permitted to snuff out any semblance of individual rights, not only when there was an abortion, but *even when there was none and none had been attempted.*

As Goldberg perceptively points out, the re-casting of laws to define embryos or fetuses as "people," or "children," has "resulted in women being punished for things they do or don't do while pregnant." She mentioned another case, this one in Alabama, in which a woman was charged with "chemical endangerment of a child," because she twice took half a Valium while pregnant.

In 2014, the Alabama Supreme Court upheld the conviction of a woman who took cocaine while pregnant, despite having delivered a completely healthy child. Between 2006 and 2020, National Advocates for Pregnant Woman identified 1,254 such injustices, Goldberg notes. She quotes Lynn Paltrow of the National Advocates: "The effort to add fetuses to the Constitution is increasingly an idea to justify essentially removing the constitutional rights of pregnant people." There already is a push by some ignorant conservatives to do away with "birthright citizenship," which would deny citizenship to those born in this country based on the status of their parents. These are people who are carried away by hostility to immigrants and to racial or religious groups different from themselves. They obviously fail to understand the clear language of the Fourteenth Amendment, but it is consistent with the behavior of tyrants throughout history who inflict punishment on people because of enmity toward their parents.

It would be difficult for even the most brilliant writer to put it more accurately, powerfully, or presciently than Goldberg. "Poolaw's case," she wrote, "is an injustice, but it also is a warning. This is what happens when the law treats embryos and fetuses as people with rights that supersede the rights of those who carry them." Sadly, it would be foolish to expect that reasoned arguments could ever persuade abortion opponents to rethink their positions. On the other hand, many opponents have suspended their opposition, and will continue to do so, for as long as it takes to secure an abortion for a clandestine mistress, or for a family member with a troublesome or otherwise unwanted pregnancy.

So it is not correct that the United States has had a tradition of abortion prohibition, while simultaneously being a "free country." The association of anti-abortion policies with right-wing authoritarianism is definite. Whether there is a cause-and-effect relationship is irrelevant. All repressive, dictatorial, policies need to be opposed.

As an aside: requiring vaccination or requiring a face mask for the public health is no more repressive than outlawing public nudity. A government that can legitimately require one to wear pants in public (or helmets for cyclists and seat belts for those in an auto) also has the authority to require a face mask to protect oneself and others.

This is not to dismiss America's traditional affection for the ideals of freedom, nor the splendid assertions of our admirable Declaration of Independence, but to point out that their implementation is shockingly incomplete. As Ales Debeljiak, the Slovenian poet who also is a thoughtful and insightful commentator on America's political system, and its arts and culture, notes, both fascism and capitalism destroy civil society, and turn isolated individuals into passive spectators. Nevertheless, "it is an error to consider the two 'systems of domination' as equivalent."[8] Always keep in mind Winston Churchill's comment, something to the effect that democracy is the worst form of government…..except for all the others.

To all those who, rather than seeking true reform, support the most disruptive candidates, naively believing that chaos will bring revolution and utopia, be careful what you wish for. Chaos simply brings more chaos, and repression

---

8   See Max J. Skidmore, "Review of *Reluctant Modernity: The Institution of Art and Its Historical Forms*, Lanham, MD: Rowman and Littlefield, 1998; in Joey Skidmore, *The Review as Art and Communication*, London: Cambridge Scholars' Publishing, 2013, pp. 74-75.

CHAPTER SIX

CONSIDERING THE CONSTITUTIONALISM OF WOMEN'S RIGHTS, INCLUDING REPRODUCTIVE RIGHTS

The language of the Constitution is plain in its protection of rights, and has no provision that excludes women (the Fifteenth Amendment that eliminates race as a criterion for voting does limit its protection to men, but the Nineteenth Amendment that eliminates sex as a criterion supersedes the Fifteenth's limitation; the amendments thus need to be considered together). A politicized court can rule otherwise, that is, it could rule to limit women's rights, only by ignoring or rationalizing away the Constitution's clear meaning.

For example, it is wrong to say that an anti-abortion law places no undue burden on a woman because it does not require a woman to raise the child; she can always give the child up for adoption (as Justice Barrett speculated, supporting "safe harbor" laws that permit women to abandon infants at certain locations without fear of prosecution). It is well to protect such a woman from prosecution, of course, but that cold-hearted approach used as an excuse to ban abortion ignores the coercion that requires her to carry a pregnancy to term and to give birth—hardly insignificant impositions. It also ignores the grief that might result from a bond that might have developed between the woman and her infant, even though she had not wanted the baby. Thus, such a ruling would ignore the protections that the Constitution provides for women.

When anyone, especially a large segment of the population, has complete power to make decisions for their own bodies taken away by government, there is only one proper definition to be applied: slavery. That argument is rarely encountered[1]—though it would seem obvious—but surely the Thirteenth Amendment, the amendment that outlaws slavery, ensures a woman's right to decide what she does with her own body. "Neither slavery nor involuntary servitude . . . shall exist within the United States," seems rather straightforward. There is an exception for those convicted of crime, but getting pregnant is not a criminal act. Can anyone doubt that there would be an enormous outcry if government were to take away men's rights to control their own bodily functions?

Before *Roe*, abortion had gone from an accepted procedure, to one with restrictions, and then, in the twentieth century, to one that to a large extent had been banned in the United States. This had happened virtually without consultation and certainly without participation from those affected: women. The Thalidomide outrage and notoriety of Sherri Finkbine's highly publicized experience helped bring about the ruling that reconsidered women's rights, *Roe* v. *Wade*.

For what it's worth, despite the theories and the assurances of anti-regulation economists, who have strongly influenced the Republican Party, the "free market" did not act to drive the company that developed and aggressively marketed Thalidomide out of business, even though its actions caused horrendous tragedies. If reality mattered to them, assuming they were at least minimally informed about American history, such economists and their Republican followers would have known better. Another example bears repeating: the company that mixed a safe, antibacterial, sulfa drug into a solvent known to be poisonous in order to create "Elixir Sulfanilamide," to be taken orally, killed over 100 people in 1937. Regardless, it disclaimed responsibility, and remained in the industry.

---

1   Elie Mystal, a lawyer and political writer for *The Nation*, also has made the argument.

There is no denying the enormous pressures on Finkbine, or the anguish that she endured. Abortion prohibitions in pre-*Roe* days certainly created hardships for women across the board, but those hardships were not evenly distributed—nor will they be if the Court moves to reinstate the ability of states to restrict women's reproductive rights. Abortion for ordinary women, without Finkbine's wealth or celebrity status, often involved attempts to achieve termination by self-medication, or to seek it from illicit and dangerous practitioners. Practically speaking, for most women there were almost no legal, safe, alternatives. The results too often were tragic.

Fortuitously, just as this chapter was underway, the *Kansas City Star* published an extraordinary, and extensive, account of what it was like, immediately before *Roe*, to secure a legal, safe, abortion in the United States.[2] This was an example of excellent journalism from a newspaper that, along with most others, has shrunk through the years. Unlike most others, though the *Star* continues to maintain a tradition of superb investigative reporting.

The article deals with Pam Mattox, who in 1972 was an 18-year-old college student. She knew little about sex, birth control, or reproduction. Just as her boyfriend was being shipped off to the military, she discovered that she was pregnant. He wanted to keep the baby, but she had never wanted children, and had other plans for her life. He honored her wishes, and helped as he could.

She had few options, all frightening. She could have secured a legal abortion in Kansas, one of the rare states that permitted it under limited circumstances, but the law at the time required three doctors to certify that it was necessary for her mental well being. Moreover, because she was under 21, she would have to have the consent of her parents. This, she said, was impossible. Her violent, alcoholic, controlling, father would have beaten her, possibly to death.

2   Katie Bernard, "I've Never Regretted It," *Kansas City Star* (Jan. 9, 2022), pp. 11A-13A.

She could have sought an illegal, and dangerous, abortion in Kansas. She could have changed her life plans, quit college, and become a teenaged, unwed, mother and been an outcast, the target of scorn, considering the stigma at the time. Finally, she could fly across the country to Washington, D.C. and obtain a legal, confidential, abortion in a safe hospital. She chose the latter.

Her boyfriend managed to secure the money (roughly a full month's pay for a Marine at the time), and quickly she found herself, in the middle of the night, alone and afraid, somewhere in Washington, D.C. She found a security guard who called a cab to take her to her hotel. The cab fare meant that she had no lunch the next day. The next morning she had the procedure, and received sound (and welcome) information regarding birth control. The information also enlightened her regarding reproduction.

She flew back to Kansas City that evening. Her college roommate's boyfriend, who had taken her to the airport, was there to pick her up. She had been away for 24 hours. Mattox remembers the experience as the most traumatic of her life, but said that, even so, it enabled her to feel free.

As traumatic as this was for her, things were far worse for most women of the time with unwanted pregnancies. Mattox determined to devote her career to assisting women who needed abortion services. Her boyfriend's Vietnam experience had damaged him. He returned with PTSD and an abusive streak, the marriage did not occur, and the relationship ended. Now, a half century later, Mattox is a member of Grandmothers for Reproductive Rights. She looks back at her abortion—and at her career assisting women with unwanted pregnancieswithout a hint of regret.

There is little question, though, of the fervent preoccupation anti-abortionists often develop. Rhetoric is powerful. Calling abortion murder, and repeating it constantly, is powerful enough to generate strong emotion for those who accept anti-abortion rhetoric.

Calling it murder of little children, is even worse. Certainly, many women are present in the anti-abortion cause, but the cause seems to appeal especially to those who are not affected, but who wish to control women. Those who have experienced demonstrations at Planned Parenthood locations, for example, tend to be struck by how many of the demonstrators—many observers, in fact, never see an exception—are elderly white men. American anti-abortionists who become terrorists, those who assassinate doctors who perform abortions, or who bomb medical clinics that perform abortion, are virtually all white men.

To demonstrate the tendency toward obsession that the subject of abortion arouses, and also its affinity with right wing extremist views, consider the author of *Vindicating Lincoln: Defending the Politics of our Greatest President.* This is especially relevant, as I shall make clear, because of the tendency of anti-abortionists to trumpet loudly that abortion is tantamount to slavery—when actually the opposite is true. That author, Thomas Krannawitter, writes quite well, and produces a superb analysis of Lincoln, defending the sixteenth president, the greatest president of all,[3] against various charges from right and left: that he was a tyrant, that he actually was uninterested in slavery, that he was a racist with no concern for Americans of African descent, that Lincoln began the "deterioration" of American government, and its tumbling into all that the right finds unconstitutional, even evil (such as programs to ease the lives of the downtrodden), making the country "statist" (meaning it functions as though government has some utility), and all the nonsense charges thrown about from Lincoln haters, usually from the south, but including some from elsewhere.

---

3   The bombastic braggart Trump, who attempts to cover his incompetence by claiming to be the best at anything and everything, claims to be the best of all the presidents, but even he concedes that he is the best "with the possible exception of Lincoln." This may have been after he belatedly discovered, to his astonishment, that Lincoln was a Republican; most people don't know that, he said.

Krannawitter is himself an adherent of extremist views. These are characteristic of many of his fellow Straussians (students of the late political philosopher Leo Strauss, and students of those students). Straussians form the nucleus of the "neoconservatives," so prominent in the disastrous foreign policies of former President George W. Bush, including the invasion of Iraq. Prominent Straussians, in fact, in their Project for a New American Century, had urged such an invasion on President Clinton considerably before Bush took office.[4] Being wiser as well as less reckless than Bush (at least in his official policies), Clinton rebuffed their efforts.

In Strauss's defense, "Straussian" politics are not always consistent with those of Strauss himself. in Krannawitter's case, he is a "West Coast Straussian," having come from Claremont Graduate University, as opposed to the group with somewhat different views out of the University of Chicago. (Disclaimer, I had five graduate courses from one of Strauss's prominent students, and thus have some familiarity with the subject.)[5]

Happily, Krannawitter's analyses of Lincoln's thought do not reflect his extreme views; in fact, Krannawitter is capable of superb analyses, as he demonstrates in his material on Lincoln. Unhappily, he cannot resist digressing into contemporary politics, and anti-abortion rants, even in a book set more than a century and a half earlier, and far remote from the ideological preoccupations of American conservatives.

I dealt with this in 2010, and my comments then are relevant now to current discussions of conservatism, and of abortion and informed common sense.[6] Krannawitter, sophisticated and excellent

4   Max J. Skidmore, "Advancing Toward Science: Retreating From Responsibility?" in Max J. Skidmore and Biko Koenig, eds., *Anti-Poverty Measures in America: Scientism and Other Obstacles,* Washington: Westphalia Press, 2019, pp. 91-109; on Straussians, see pp. 100-107; on PNAC, see pp. 105-107.

5   For a witty introduction into Straussianism, see Anne Norton, *Leo Strauss and the Politics of American Empire,* New Haven: Yale University Press, 2004.

6   Max J. Skidmore, "Antebellum American Thought and Politics," *Journal of*

analyst though he can be, adheres to some simplistic ideas that
affect his views of social welfare, abortion, and the like. He is out-
raged by taxation, because it "confiscates private property." Therefore, it leaves the individual with "less ability to determine what
and how to spend."

This should be recognized as too simplistic to be taken seriously. In
fact, "often the economic situation of the country, hence the ability of its residents to spend as they see fit, has been greater during
times of high taxation than when taxes are low." There are many
examples of this, but writing in 2010, I provided the example that,
"disposable income was considerably greater for Americans in general during the Clinton years, with higher taxes, than during the
Bush years, with lower taxes. In fact, after an orgy of tax reductions
under Bush II, the economy went into a free fall that destroyed
some $5 trillion, causing it simply to vanish. That certainly restrict-
ed people's ability to spend far more than, say, the FICA tax for
Social Security has or ever could."

Krannawitter extols—in a book on Lincoln!—"The days of "economic growth and prosperity under Presidents Warren Harding
and Calvin Coolidge," and argues that these flowed from the res-
toration of balanced budgets, and "limited, constitutional, government." He does not mention that "the 1920s, of course, ended with
the worst financial disaster in American history, the Great Depres-
sion." He very likely is completely unaware that recessions tend to
follow balanced budgets. Surely, though, he knows, but does not
mention, the prosperity under President Clinton, let alone under
Presidents Truman, Eisenhower, Kennedy, and Johnson. Again, in
a book on Lincoln, he condemns "federal regulatory power as beyond what any 'commonsense reading of the Constitution could
ever explain.'" That sort of reasoning is why I stress that "common
sense," must be *informed* common sense.

American Culture, 33:1 (March 2010).

Directly relevant to contemporary controversies on abortion, whatever Lincoln might have thought on the subject—in the unlikely event he ever did think about it—"Krannawitter even asserts that opposition to abortion is equivalent to opposition to slavery; each counters inappropriate assertions of 'choice.' One need not take a position on abortion, though, to recognize the limitation of this argument. In ascribing a full range of human rights to a potential human being, he denies them to a fully-functioning, existing, human being, whom he denies the freedom to control even her own body—that is, whom he would enslave. Thus, his opposition to slavery seems curiously incomplete. If he is to oppose abortion effectively, he should develop a more reasonable argument—although it would be better left to a different work, not included gratuitously in a vindication of Lincoln."[7]

Roe v. *Wade* in 1973 substantially changed the situation regarding abortion in the United States. The Texas law that was being challenged made abortion illegal, unless a doctor certified that it was necessary to save the woman's life. A very young lawyer, Sarah Weddington, only 26, argued the case for the plaintiff, "Jane Doe" (Norma McCorvey), who at the time remained anonymous. Weddington argued that the state's statute was unconstitutional, because it infringed upon her client's right of privacy. She cited five amendments, the First, Fourth, Fifth, Ninth and Fourteenth, as protecting that right.

The Court ruled, 7 to 2, that it did. There is a fundamental right to privacy in the Fourteenth Amendment, the majority opinion said, and the balance of a woman's right to an abortion against a state's right to protect women's health and the "potentiality of human life," changes at various stages of the pregnancy. In the first trimester, the state may not restrict a woman's right to choose an abortion. In the second trimester, the state may impose restrictions that are reasonably related to the woman's health. In the third tri-

---

7   *Ibid.*

mester, after viability, the state may impose any restriction, providing that it allows for exceptions required for the life or health of the mother. The Texas law did not make any allowances for various stages of the pregnancy, and therefore it violated a woman's right to privacy.

Despite a flood of criticism, the tripartite formulation that *Roe* set forth is reasonable. The closer the birth, the more justifiable it may be to place restrictions on abortion; not only is fetal development greater, but the woman has had more time to decide. There must be a time, a considerable time (regardless of diversionary tactics such as "fetal 'heartbeat' and the like), during which abortion must completely be at the option of the pregnant woman, guided by medical advice. Regardless of the bleats of protest that the Constitution does not mention "privacy," and the like, there is a plethora of rights universally conceded that the Constitution fails to mention specifically. Such a fundamentalist interpretation of the Constitution, an overly literal interpretation, ignores the plain language that has been in the Constitution ever since ratification of the Bill of Rights. It bears repetition that the Ninth Amendment obliterates the fundamentalist—and unconstitutional—approach that assumes the Constitution must mention every right: "The enumeration in the Constitution, of certain rights, shall not be construed to deny or disparage others retained by the people." Note that the language refers only to "the people," not to the states.

What the Constitution does, indeed, mention specifically, is that slavery is prohibited. The Thirteenth Amendment says clearly and definitively that "neither slavery nor involuntary servitude shall exist, except as punishment for crime whereof the party shall have duly convicted, shall exist within the United States, or any place subject to their jurisdiction."

Broadly speaking, the dictionary definition of slavery is "a state of subjection." A synonym is "Involuntary subjection to another or others."[8] When government officials, whether or not authorized by law, determine that a woman must carry a pregnancy to term, regardless of her wishes, her volition, that removes the woman's ability to make decisions regarding her pregnancy, and places that woman directly within a condition that meets the stated definition of slavery.

Sarah Weddington's argument before the Court in *Roe,* that abortion prohibitions infringe upon a woman's right to privacy guaranteed by numerous amendments to the Constitution, The First, Fourth, Fifth, Ninth, and Fourteenth was brilliant. That argument now is under attack from those who disagree, as it has been since the Court accepted it. Typical of the characteristics of the attacks was the article mentioned earlier in Chapter One by Bryan Hughes, the Texas state senator who claims authorship of the strongly anti-abortion Texas Senate Bill 8. Hughes called the right to abortion a "fantasy spun by the ludicrous logic of *Roe* v. *Wade.*" This is a classic illustration of constitutional fundamentalism.

Nevertheless, *Roe* has been the bedrock of reproductive rights, although the Court has steadily chipped away at its protections. Among many instances were *Harris* v. *McRae* in 1980 that upheld the notorious Hyde amendment that has banned appropriated federal funds from being used for abortions; and *Planned Parenthood* v. *Casey* in 1992 that upheld *Roe,* but permitted Pennsylvania to impose restrictions, such as a 24-hour waiting period, and a requirement for counselling.

The argument regarding the Thirteenth Amendment, bolstered by the Ninth, complements the argument from privacy. It can serve as a complement, or it can stand alone as the complete argument. In either case, both arguments recognize the rights of the pregnant woman. All arguments in support of eliminating abortions

---

8   "Slavery," in *Webster's New Universal Unabridged Dictionary* (Based on the Second Edition of *The Random House Dictionary of the English Language*).

rest on completely ignoring the woman's rights to self-determination—her right to be free; not to be enslaved—or on a manufactured assumption of fetal rights that supersede any rights of the woman. An enlightened Court should eliminate the decisions that weakened *Roe's* protections, and far from overturning *Roe*, should adopt expanded rights recognizing women's constitutional rights to be free from enslavement.

There is little hope that the current, corrupted, Court will accept this logic, or maintain protections for a woman's reproductive rights. Constitutional expert Geoffrey Richard Stone wrote a compelling analysis of the Supreme Court in the 21st century. He demonstrated conclusively that the Court has become far more conservative in recent decades; that the conservatives are *far* more conservative than their predecessors, and the liberals are only *moderately* liberal. Stevens, Souter, Ginsburg, Breyer, Sotomayor, and Kagan, he says "are nowhere near as liberal as justices like Brennan, Warren, Marshall, and Douglas. They have not been nearly as extreme in their liberalism as recent conservative justices have been in their conservatism. Moreover, the two so-called swing justices in recent years (O'Connor and Kennedy) have in fact been quite conservative, though not as extreme in their conservatism as Rehnquist, Scalia, Roberts, and Alito." The conservatives, he notes, "have played fast-and-loose with the law in order to reach the outcomes they prefer." The selective activism, as he terms it, "cannot be explained by any principled theory of constitutional interpretation." Instead, the justices in the conservative majority give every indication that they operate on "their prejudices and their respective pasts and self-conscious desires." Their decisions are based on a "set of personal and ideological preferences about such matters as guns, corporations, gays, commercial activity, religion," and the like."[9]

---

9   Geoffrey Richard Stone, "The Supreme Court in the 21st Century," *Daedalus*,
     142:2 (Spring 2013) https://search.yahoo.com/yhs/search?hspart=trp&h

The astonishing thing about Stone's perceptive article, is that it sounds so current, yet it was published years ago, in 2013. That was long before Trump was a major fixture on the political scene, and far before he had any influence on the Court. At that time, the Court already had been corrupted by decades of Federalist-Society-influenced Republican extremism. Trump's three appointments have escalated the zealotry, and were achieved with dramatic, and openly public, trampling on accepted procedures. McConnell denied President Obama his constitutional right to have his nomination to fill Justice Scalia's vacant seat considered by the Senate, and no Republican objected. Kavanaugh's confirmation was after he manifestly displayed a lack of judicial temperament, and Barrett's confirmation was rushed through in direct violation of what McConnell had used as his excuse not to consider Obama's nominee. The current Court is much more extreme, far worse, than it was at the time of Stone's alarming analysis.

As the superb Court analyst, Linda Greenhouse, has written, the three Trump justices are doing exactly what they were appointed to do, and the Court itself has been "weaponized." In cases dealing with campaign finance, the new majority is "weaponizing the First Amendment to serve its anti-labor agenda." Despite their pious protestations during their hearings, the new justices are complicit in overturning precedent, leaving abortion clinics in Texas "all but shuttered for months." That is a harbinger of things to come. Women's reproductive rights are in danger of being thrust back into the back alley, where their only options are dangerous and illegal; that is, they will no longer be rights at all. The same is true for religious education and the separation of church and state. These are all being accomplished not because cases are normally working their way to the Court, but because the extremist justices now have the power to choose obscure cases from a huge pool that fit

simp=yhs-001&grd=1&type=Y149_F163_202167_081020&p=Stone%2C+The+Supreme+Court+in+the+21st+ (retrieved 13 January 2022).

their rigid ideology. As for abortion, they chose an unlikely case, because it offered "a vehicle the newly empowered anti-abortion supermajority was waiting for." Greenhouse notes that over history, the Court changes, but it does so incrementally. That change, she wrote, during Trump years, "arrived in a torrent."[10]

This has resulted in a sharp decline in confidence in the Court, and it could destroy it in the long run. What is needed, is the appointment of four to six new justices, expanding the Court to "unpack" it and restore balance. With Democratic strength in the Senate at 50, one of which is the conservative Democrat from West Virginia, Joe Manchin, and another is the notoriously flaky Kyrsten Sinema, from Arizona, the likelihood of positive change prior to the midterm elections borders on nil. At the moment, the indications and historical trends are unfavorable, making leaders bemoan and pundits issue dire warnings. Considering the strange nature of contemporary politics, though, and that at this writing the elections are roughly ten months away, many changes can occur. Democrats and thoughtful independents must work as though their lives depend on the outcome, because in a very real sense they do.

Vote for Democrats at all levels, and work in every way possible to defeat any Republican at any level. With a decent Democratic majority after the midterms, there would be a true chance for a progressive revolution, and that certainly would bring protection for a woman's reproductive rights.

---

10   Linda Greenhouse, "The Supreme Court, Weaponized," *New York Times Sunday Review* (December 19, 2022), p. 2.

CHAPTER SEVEN

PROTECTION FROM THE PERSONAL TO THE POLITICAL*

In view of the nature of this book, dealing with abortion, which is a subject relating mainly to women, with direct effects *only* on women, I have decided to revise an appendix from *The Common Sense Manifesto* to be included here as well. Anti-abortion measures are direct, and misogynistic, forces aimed at women. Women need to be aware of the political force they can bring to protect themselves from all such forces. Hostile physical forces exist also for nearly everyone, but to a substantial, and unfortunate, degree, women are the most likely to be targets for predators. The information in this chapter is applicable to everyone, but especially to women.

In a civilized world, part of the social contract is that government is responsible for providing safety. It stands as a shield against foreign threats, against dangerous products and environmental pollutants, and against threatened harm from domestic sources such as criminals. Self-protection thus should not be required.

Unfortunately, threats to our well-being have never been completely eliminated, despite the efforts of government even when it is at its best, so it always has been prudent to be prepared. This does not mean to be paranoid, but to be alert. Even less does it mean that victims should be blamed for being victims. Being inadequately prepared may place one at greater risk, but in no way should anyone infer that full blame should be laid anywhere but at the feet of bullies and oppressors.

Small-government ideologues who in America call themselves

---

* Adapted from "Fighting is Wrong; Learn to Fight," *Common Sense Manifesto,* Washington: Westphalia Press, 2020

"conservatives" have brought about conditions that increase risk for the people. Recent Republican measures have considerably reduced environmental protections. Even the air we breathe and the water we drink can no longer be free from reasonable suspicion that it may be harming us. When Republicans of today are in control, the situation will assuredly become worse. Protecting yourself against these threats may even be impossible. Nevertheless, we must all be alert to protecting ourselves as much as possible from pollution, contaminated food, environmental pathogens, and unhealthy lifestyles. Vigilance, vaccination, prudent precautions regarding sanitation, and the like are essential. These days such precautions also involve social distancing and mask wearing. Political action is always necessary, but never more so than currently

There are also other threats that are more immediate, and certainly more dramatic. Under pressure from the National Rifle Association, Republicans—some gleefully, and others reluctantly—at all levels of government for decades have rushed to do the bidding of arms manufacturers and the NRA to welcome rapid-fire, enormous capacity, high velocity weapons, and other weapons of varying characteristics into public, as well as domestic, spaces.

Common-sense controls on firearms have been so reduced by misinterpreting the Second Amendment—misinterpretations accepted by a newly-compliant Supreme Court, overturning tradition and advancing the NRA's apocalyptic dreams—that the deadliest weapons are available virtually anywhere, to virtually anyone. The fanatic cry of NRA spokesman, the ineffable Wayne LaPierre, that "only a good guy with a gun" can provide protection, is ridiculous; the preposterous proposition advanced by NRA henchmen that "the more guns, the less violence" not only offends common sense, but has made the United States the country most widely known for death by firearm.

It is too bad that it is not possible to prosecute the agents of death as war criminals; they are indirectly responsible for more slaughter than overt terrorists. Deaths include not only suicide, domestic violence, police and vigilante shootings of unarmed civilians—largely black males, vengeful killings by individuals and general adherents of the gun culture, but they also include mass deaths. Sadly, the United States easily holds world-wide records as the country with the most frequent mass murder of innocents, most often committed by racist ideologues.

There was recently a request from deep within the NRA that made it quite obvious that when there are too many guns available, a "good guy" who has one is hardly sufficient to protect anyone. LaPierre attempted to persuade the NRA to provide him with an armed and fortified mansion for protection against alleged threats on his life. By so doing, he implicitly admitted that he considered his protection to require far more than his ability to carry a gun. Thus, his solution to individual protection is not conceal-carry; it is to have a fortified (luxury, of course) mansion. Admittedly, that would probably be more effective than NRA slogans, but it is so absurd and so expensive that the NRA turned down his self-serving request.

Firearms aside, the culture is becoming more accepting of violence. Even the former—and fortunately defeated—president of the United States notoriously urged, and urges, his supporters to give vent to their fury, once having gone so far as to say he would pay their fines should they be prosecuted. Although his supporters had and have no more chance of having him actually pay fines than tradesmen who through the years have complained that he refuses to pay them, such rhetoric from one who has been president can only be pernicious, even when it comes from a defeated politician who no longer holds office.

Common sense indicates that, at a minimum, citizens should be aware of the value of voting for a major party that supports the values of a democratic republic. Unfortunately, of America's two major parties, only one, the Democratic Party, now supports such values.

Modern Republicans seek to undermine them at every turn, and, regarding women, are actively anti-abortion. All Americans should understand the laws governing them, and what agencies can assist them if necessary. They should know of the elected officials who make policy and how to communicate with those officials. They should know what situations to avoid, what actions to take in any situation they are likely to encounter, and they should know how to respond to actual physical assault. Obviously, there is little that you can do to fend off a bullet if someone is making you a target. The best strategy is to anticipate, and, if at all possible to avoid it and not to be in a dangerous situation. It is decidedly *not* to carry a firearm. In a situation of mass shooting, having a firearm could at times be of help, but it is far more likely that the one who is armed will be the first to be shot.

Domestic situations, and personal situations in general, must be improved. What could be more sad, or more deserving of remedy, than personal relations that contain plausible elements of fear? Relationships of trust must replace those of danger. Remedies must involve broad and widespread education in empathy—and in common sense. They also may involve appeals to shame and decency. For better or worse, they also should include development of skills in self-defense. Consider the truth that, sadly, remains in the comment often attributed to Margaret Atwood: Men are afraid women will laugh at them; women are afraid men will kill them.

Physical skills are important, and although it requires work to develop them, they can be achieved more easily than it might seem. Mental skills are at least equally important. There are a number of works on self-defense that can be helpful. Looking only at one source: that newspaper of record, the Grey Lady herself, the *New York Times*, reveals that even there in that staid venue, there have been numerous articles through the years on self-defense for women.

Men should not make the mistake of dismissing these as "merely women's articles." Techniques that are valuable for women are equally valuable for men. Regardless of how formidable a man may be, he can always encounter someone more formidable. Regardless of how formidable a man may be, under the right conditions he can be bested by a smaller, weaker, victim who is determined, trained, and willing to do what is necessary without hesitation. Being prepared for self-defense requires both men and women to be able to function well when threatened by someone larger and stronger. Women, too, should be admonished not to assume that they are helpless when facing someone regardless of size and strength. Albeit in different ways, women can be equally formidable with men.

In an aptly-titled article, "Like a Tupperware Party, With Punching," The Times in 2012 discussed self-defense courses for women. The author, Linda Himelstein, noted that such courses are most successful when presented in an appealing manner, not merely as self-defense. She quoted Lisa Skvarla, the head of "the American Women Self Defense Association and a creator of Girls' Fight Night Out" that it is necessary to "do something" to make women want to attend classes. Leanne Brecklin, a criminologist, conducted research that supported this; she found that "sharing women's success stories" is an effective tool. "Fighting back," Brecklin noted, "is not only possible but also effective." Courses can be aimed specifically toward certain groups, such as Jerrett Arthur's "Mothers Against Malicious Acts," which teaches not only self-protection, but also "protecting one's children" (Jarrett has a black belt in Krav Maga, the self-defense art of the Israeli military).[1] Her organization is called MAMA. That would be far better on a ball cap than the MAGA slogan that often infects them today.

The world has been shocked in recent years by publicity from India. It took many outrageous acts before the dangers to women in the subcontinent received publicity outside its borders. Especially in certain areas, such as Delhi, sexual harassment has been rampant

---

1   Linda Himelstein, "Like a Tupperware Party, With Punching," The New York Times, (July 26, 2012), E 5.

for decades, if not centuries. The euphemism "eve teasing" covers everything from catcalls, to rape and murder.[2] The New Delhi police force for a decade or so has been offering free instruction to girls in the city's public schools and universities. Women police constables are the instructors, and the courses include effective techniques from various martial arts. They also offer Summer and Winter camps for women, and "gender sensitization" courses for boys, "a lawyer-led course that teaches men how to help women in trouble and how to be more respectful to them in public spaces." A woman instructor, a constable, said it aims to develop feelings of responsibility among men for their conduct, so that they will "feel responsible towards girls and women."[3]

The first thing the Indian girls learn is contrary to their cultural deference. They scream to attract help. Then, they fight. As a result of the increase in publicity, even internationally, and of newly-energized women's organizations, women are beginning to be heard. Indian women now are coming forth to file complaints, and sometimes they find officials willing to listen, and to act.

In early 2019, the *Times* published an article cautioning women not to succumb to fear, but to be prudent when traveling. The safety tips included many common-sense recommendations (carry wedges for door stops to keep doors securely closed, etc.), and among them are "learn to defend yourself."[4] This is so important

---

2   I learned about this national shame—certainly a vicious cousin to another vicious practice, bride-burning—when I lived in India as a Distinguished Fulbright Lecturer, and was CEO of a large research library in Hyderabad, the American Studies Research Centre; this was before these pernicious practices were widely known outside of India.

3   Maria Abi-Habib, "'Men Treat Us Like We Aren't Human.' Indian Girls Learn to Fight Back," *The New York Times* (April 16, 2018); https://www.nytimes.com/2018/04/16/world/asia/india-girls-self-defense.html; (accessed November 6, 2019).

4   Tariro Mzezewa and Lela Moore, "'Don't Succumb to the Fear' Women Share Travel Safety Tips," *The New York Times* (March 26, 2019); https://www.nytimes.com/2019/03/26/travel/safety-tips-female-solo-travel.html; (ac-

that it can hardly be overstressed. Women should learn to use any available object as a weapon. They should trust their instincts, and not hesitate to summon help. They should not be frightened to be alone, and they should continue to travel!

In a vivid presentation of personal experience learning to fight, the *Times* published, "Beth Ditto is 'Feeling Self-Defensive' and Fights Back." The core of the course it describes seeks to eliminate women's feeling of powerlessness. It concentrates on a few key techniques for breaking free, and teaches striking back. "Eyes! Knees; Groin: Throat!" becomes the chant, stressing the most effective—and devastating—targets that also require the least skill. "'As a fat person, rolling around on the ground, I think that's really cool, too,' Ms. Ditto Said."[5]

For anyone who wishes to see examples of fighting techniques that enable women to defeat men—anyone who can tolerate scenes of extreme violence, that is—there is an extraordinary film, *Atomic Blonde*. Ignore the title, and concentrate on the inspired performance of the superb Charlize Theron. She typically immerses herself in her roles, and this instance is no exception; she trained vigorously for many months, all the while seeking realism regarding the fighting techniques that are most appropriate for women.

She found those techniques, and presents them thoroughly. A surprising amount of the film consists of her character successfully fighting off attackers. The fighting is realistic; in no way does she escape unscathed. An early scene shows her weary, exhausted in fact, in a tub of ice water with floating ice cubes, soothing her bruised and battered body. As the review in *The Guardian* put it, there are "some terrifically good one-on-one combat scenes—much more continuously and realistically shot than the rest of the film—crun-

cessed November 9, 2019).

5   Alexis Soloski, "Beth Ditto is 'Feeling Self-Defensive' and Fights Back," *The New York Times* (November 3, 2019), ST 4.

chily horrible extended punch-ups in which Theron establishes some serious martial arts chops."[6]

A personal note may be appropriate here. I was impressed by Theron's performance, and I have studied martial arts for more than a half century, having earned advanced black belts (5th and 6th degrees) in several styles. The *Guardian* review I cite here also used the word "prurient" to describe the bathtub scene, but that is nonsense. The scene graphically demonstrated the damage that combat inflicts upon the human body, was integral to the material, and contained not a hint of the erotic.

The most effective of the numerous self-defense training courses primarily for women, at least according to reputation and descriptions of the training, may be Model Mugging (note: I know it only by reputation, and have not personally observed any of their sessions). It involves sound training, with hard and vigorous pummeling of well-padded instructors. It seems to be scientifically grounded, and philosophically appropriate. Although Model Mugging is not a martial art itself, it seems to be compatible with various forms of martial arts training, and would seem to be highly effective in developing skills specifically in self-defense. As a public service, Model Mugging has posted a rather extensive list of self-defense articles.[7]

Among numerous books on self-defense, one especially designed for women is noteworthy. Shelley Klingerman's *Vigilance* takes a holistic approach.[8] Quite appropriately, she sets the scene, discusses not only the need to be vigilant, but what it involves. She warns

---

6   Peter Bradshaw, "Atomic Blonde Review—Charlize Theron Punches Up Hyperactively Silly Thriller," (August 9, 2017); https://www.theguardian.com/film/2017/aug/09/atomic-blonde-review-charlize-theron-punches-up-hyperactively-silly-thriller; (accessed November 10, 2019).

7   See "Self-Defense Articles," *Model Mugging* http://modelmugging.org/self-defense-articles/; (accessed November 10, 2019).

8   Shelley Klingerman, *Vigilance*, Indianapolis, Niche Pressworks, 2019.

that it is essential to be prepared to face fears; waiting until one is in a dangerous situation is ineffective. Fear paralyzes, but knowing what to do can be a protection against its debilitating effect. Training can enable one to discard any thought of being "ladylike," and—however off-putting it may be to some—instead to be "a warrior." She calls upon her readers to "join the community of bad-ass women," and launches into her first chapter, perfectly summed up in its title, "Prepare—Prevent—Protect."

Klingerman's book is rich in detail, and strong on connection to actual situations. She outlines everyday objects that can be used as weapons, she gives useful pointers on personal protection and prudent measures to take to reduce danger while abroad or at home in familiar surroundings. There is far too much to summarize, but it would be well for her book to be widely read and heeded.

Literally, on the very day that I have been reviewing this manuscript to send to the publisher—the 18th of January, 2022—the *New York Times* and other newspapers around the county carried the happy report that hostages in a Texas synagogue escaped their captor. An intruder, armed with an arsenal including an AR-15 automatic weapon, had held them prisoner for hours. Finally, when the time was appropriate and they saw an opportunity, they fought back. The rabbi threw a chair at the gunman, the captors fought back, and escaped. There was certainly no "good man with a gun," and they were not rescued or released. They fought their way out, and all escaped unharmed.

The rabbi, Charlie Cytron-Walker, credited security and self-defense training that he and his congregation had received. It enabled them to take effective measures even against a heavily-armed adversary, and to survive without injury. The rabbi and the hostages did precisely what this chapter recommends. They received training, they were prepared, and when an emergency took place, they were able to use the knowledge and skills that they possessed from their training to handle the situation perfectly, and to survive.

Women and men, individuals and groups, all can develop the ability to employ skills that may make the difference in a variety of threatening situations. The rabbi and his congregation did so, and they serve as a lesson to all. They deserve praise.

Beyond that, there are measures that every adult citizen should be able to take to make dramatic improvements in everyday lives. Vote for candidates who are concerned for the people, rather than for their own re-election, or for their contributors.

Vote a straight ticket. Make that ticket a major party. Make that party the one that does not tolerate (let alone advocate) grabbing children from their parents at the border. Vote to remove from office anyone who does not advocate firearm control, who does not insist on control of law-enforcement violence, and who does not move effectively to protect the rights of all people, especially women. Vote consistently to reject any party that overtly or implicitly rejects the rights of women to make their own choices, whether for reproduction or any other phase of personal conduct. The House of Representatives has, with some Republican support, voted to re-authorize the lapsed Violence Against Women Act. In the Senate, the measure is stalled. Do everything you can to support re-authorization.

Direct your vote to the destruction of any party that will not move toward all measures that will improve the lives of constituents. Above all, vote to incorporate humanitarian and humane values into government, and remove all officials and members of any party that has been complicit in institutionalizing cruelty.

Targets of voters who will vote accordingly, you know who you are. Perhaps you will join many others of your party, willingly step aside, and retire from politics.

WORDS ARE IMPORTANT

A SELECTION OF RELEVANT WORDS, WITH COMMON SENSE DEFINITIONS

Abortion—Termination of a pregnancy, usually used to mean artificially induced but it can also apply to a naturally-occurring event; ie, a miscarriage; a procedure that has served to unite former enemies, Protestant Fundamentalists/Evangelicals and conservative Catholic political activists to politicize their religions; probably the most powerful symbol among religious right-wing activists, one that supersedes religious differences to create political unity.

Abortion Industry—Essentially a nonsense term that anti-abortion activists use to charge that the tiny portion of the US medical community that performs abortions does so purely to reap huge profits; it reflects an ideological stance that leads those who hold it to be unable to recognize that doctors who perform abortions have to be motivated by humanitarian concerns for women in dire circumstances. Any physician could have a substantially greater income from any other medical practice, and would not face a continual threat of assassination by fanatic, anti-abortion terrorists.

Abstinence—In relation to abortion, refraining from sexual intercourse. For many anti-abortionists, the only acceptable solution to unwanted pregnancies

Anti-Abortion—Opponents of abortion who style themselves as "Pro-Life"; obsessively concerned about life in the womb, but generally only until birth. Forced Birther would be more descriptive.

Appropriation Acts—Legislative acts authorize creation of programs, but require appropriation acts to fund them. An appropriation act provides money to operate programs already authorized. The Hyde Amendment passed Congress in 1976, and began to be attached to all appropriation acts since 1977. Hyde Amendments prohibit any federal funds from being used to provide, or facilitate, abortion.

Assassin, Assassination—Killer, killing, generally motivated by ideological purposes, usually political or religious (or both); related to abortion, assassination refers to the targeted killing by anti-abortion terrorists of medical personnel associated with abortion.

Biden, Joseph—President of the United States; he defeated the one-term former president, Donald Trump; Biden was vice president under former President Obama, also formerly was a long-time U.S. senator (chair at varied times of Senate Committee on Foreign Relations, and Senate Judiciary Committee).

Birth Control—Contraception; device or medication designed to prevent pregnancies from sexual acts. Opponents of abortion frequently oppose contraception for ideological reasons, although contraceptive use prevents abortions.

Book of Jerry Falwell—Serious study of fundamentalist language; author Susan Friend Harding identifies, and analyzes, "harmonization."

Broomfield, Charles S.—Author of "Francis A. Schaeffer: the Force Behind the Evangelical Takeover of the Republican Party in America," unpublished M.A. thesis in political science, University of Missouri-Kansas City, 2012.

Bush, George H. W.—President of the United States, vice president under Reagan, whom he succeeded in office. Father of

President George W. Bush. Opposed to abortion, friendly with religious activists. Defeated by Bill Clinton.

Bush, George W.—Son of President G. H. W. Bush; hostile to many government programs, sought to trim Social Security, opposed to abortion, a "born-again Christian" with ties to the far right. Led the country into wars, known for reckless foreign policy, and for empowering a bellicose vice president, Dick Cheney.

Catholic Church, Roman—Ancient Christian institution, sponsor of many humanitarian programs, but vigorous in opposition to contraception and abortion contributing greatly to worldwide misery. Under numerous popes, Church allied with right wing dictators; the Church is a huge institution that includes many different currents, some contradicting one another.

Child—A young human being from birth until adolescence; anti-abortionists distort the meaning to include the full gestation period, from conception to birth. Children are whole, fully-functioning, human beings, not physically attached to anyone else.

Choice—As in "pro-choice," meaning a woman's right to decide matters relating to her own body; distorted by anti-abortionists, who equate it with slavery, that is, a woman's choice for abortion, they say, is the same as a slaveholder's "choice" to own slaves; that of course is nonsense. The woman's choice is what to do with her own body; the enslaver's "choice," is what to do with *other* people's bodies (and even minds, where possible).

Christian Manifesto—Final book by Francis Schaeffer, setting out his vision for a Christian, and conservative, America; highly critical of "humanism" as including virtually all thought and practice since Darwin; starkly anti-American to the extent of being openly subversive.

Christian Reconstruction—Dominionism, following R. J. Rushdooney; calling for an aggressive and cruel Christian theocracy.

Christian Right—Segment of the American Christian community that has permitted conservative political doctrines to submerge Christian principles, in order to foster right-wing political activism (for example, it led fundamentalist/evangelicals to overlook their theological principles to support a ticket consisting of a Mormon and a Catholic, letting its political preferences for the Republican Party to overwhelm its theological opposition to Mormonism and Roman Catholicism.

Church-State Separation—Doctrine formulated powerfully in America by Roger Williams in the 17th century (the founder of Rhode Island and of the first Baptist Church in America), and by Thomas Jefferson in the 18th. Essentially, the principle is that close church-state relations lead to politicized religion and "religionized" government, corrupting both, and to repression. Ironically, Baptists, who now tend to mix church and state together and flirt with theocracy, historically were the greatest defenders of keeping church and state separate.

Conception—The act of fertilizing, creating a zygote. Many fundamentalists argue, nonsensically, that it immediately creates "personhood," which itself is an ill-defined term.

Constitutional Amendment—The formal revising of a constitution; for the Constitution of the United States, amending procedures are set forth in Article V, but only one method has ever been used: Congress proposes an amendment by a two-thirds vote of both the House and the Senate, and three-fourths of the states must ratify, either by their legislatures, or by conventions in each state. The latter procedure has been used only once, for the 21ˢᵗ Amendment repealing the 18ᵗʰ (prohibition) Amendment. Congress determines which method of ratification is to be used, and with the one exception, it has always been ratification by state legislatures. There is one other possible procedure, usually misunderstood even by people familiar with the Constitution. They believe, incorrectly, that two-thirds of the states can propose amendments, with three-fourths of the states then ratifying them. That is false. Three fourths of the states always are required for ratification, either by their legislatures, or by their specially created conventions. Proposal, though, is *always* by a national body, either Congress, or a national convention. Thus far, it has always been by the Congress. Article V does provide that two-thirds of the states can *request Congress to call a national convention to propose amendments.* That has never happened, and Congress cannot call such a convention unless two-thirds of the states request one. States can *never* propose amendments; they can only request Congress to call a convention to do so. Neither Congress nor the states can require such a national convention to consider any amendment. That would be solely up to the convention.

Constitution of the United States—the fundamental law of the country. All laws must be consistent with the Constitution. The Constitution also guarantees rights, and neither the federal government nor any state can act in a manner contrary to the Constitution.

Common Sense, Informed—The application of reason enhanced by knowledge and experience to answer a question or settle an issue.

Common Sense Manifesto—The Second in the Informed Common

Sense tetralogy, all of which identify irrational situations, and suggest reasoned remedies.

Crazy for God—Title of book by Frank Schaeffer, who, with his father, Francis, was a major influence on American fundamentalist/evangelical Protestants persuading them to discard their dismissal of abortion as a "Catholic issue," and join with Catholics in strenuous opposition to abortion; the book discusses that ideological shift, and another that led Frank Schaeffer to reject fundamentalist religion and adopt more liberal beliefs; he came to recognize that he had unleashed dangerous forces, forces that would likely target him to be among the first to be eliminated, should they ever come to power.

Crisis Pregnancy Center—Organizations designed to attract women and girls who find themselves pregnant by persuading them they will receive needed aid. However, the sole purpose of such organizations is to prevent abortion, applying whatever pressure they consider necessary to accomplish their goal.

Cult of Personality—Mass affection for a leader who is enhanced far beyond reality; generally a technique of an authoritarian government to mass its resources—media, propaganda, educational system, etc.—to strengthen its social control; the term dates from 1956 during "destalinization," and described former efforts to glorify Stalin. The contemporary Republican Party in the US elevated former President Ronald Reagan in a similar manner, until Trump superseded him as the party's new object of loyalty, affection, admiration (in Trump's case, fear fuels loyalty as much as affection does).

Dobbs v. Jackson Women's Health—Case before the Supreme Court dealing with Mississippi's harsh anti-abortion law; upholding the law likely will overturn *Roe* v. *Wade,* which is the intention of Mississippi's officials.

Enslavement—The exercise of involuntary control over the body and behavior of another person. The most extreme version, chattel slavery, was in the American south, permitting the enslaver literally to own, and even to sell, the enslaved. In modern America, forbidding abortion creates a less complete but still formidable form of enslavement by empowering government officials to force an unwilling woman against her will to carry a pregnancy to term.

Embryo—A very early stage of gestation beyond a zygote and before a fetus; categories are as much matters of definition as of biology.

Fanatic, Fanaticism—Intense, extreme, and overwhelming dedication to a specific issue to the exclusion of nuance or recognition of competing circumstances; leads frequently to violence to achieve the desired end. Most often associated with religious or political fervor. The fanatic is an extreme version of an ideologue.

First Amendment—Protects freedom of speech and religion, a free press, and the right to assemble peacefully; these imply rights to privacy in speech, expression, belief, and conduct within limits.

Fifth Amendment—Protects a right to be free from self-incrimination; protects rights to life, liberty, and property and ensures existence of private property; thus protecting several forms of privacy.

Fourteenth Amendment—Ensures equal protection before the law, and due process; creates citizenship also protects life, liberty, and property.

Fourth Amendment—Protects the home from arbitrary search and seizure; thus creates a realm of privacy.

Fetal Heartbeat Laws—Laws assuming that "heartbeat" exists early in the gestational period, and forbidding abortion as soon as the slightest electrical flutter (which the laws define as heartbeat) is detectable by the most sensitive instruments. Not scientifically valid, but an excuse to ban abortion; such laws seek to create an emotional reaction demanding that all pregnancies be carried to term

Fetus—Replaces the embryo to become the final gestational stage.

Fire Bell in the Night—Thomas Jefferson's metaphor to describe the fear for his country that the controversy regarding slavery created; abortion may be almost as divisive.

Fundamentalism—As used here, not the technical definition, but an exaggerated literalism, rigid adherence to written rules; most common in religion, but also evident elsewhere, such as in constitutional interpretation, economics, social thought, etc. Wherever it exists it tends to be accompanied by misogyny, repression, great income disparity, inflexibility, resistance to change, and inability to deal with crises.

Harding, Susan Friend—Author of *The Book of Jerry Falwell: Fundamentalist Language and Politics,* a brilliant scholarly study of fundamentalist language and practice, and calling attention to the phenomenon of "harmonization," the ability to convince oneself that logical contradiction actually can form a consistent whole.

Harmonization—The practice taught in some Bible schools that enables one to study contradictions found in scripture, and accept them both as literal truth (e.g., the two separate creation myths in Genesis, one in which God creates Adam, then other animals, and, finally Eve; and the other in which God creates whales, other animals, etc., and then Adam).

Harris v. *McRae* (1980)—Upheld the constitutionality of the Hyde

Amendment that bans the use of federal funds for abortion.

Hyde Amendment (1976)—Amendment applied to appropriation acts banning any federal funds from supporting abortion; applied since 1977.

Hyde, Henry—Republican member of the House of Representatives from Illinois, a leader in the anti-abortion movement, and author of the Hyde Amendment that from 1977 until the present (January 2022) has been attached to appropriation acts; the amendment forbids the use of any federal funds for abortions, Also a leader in the impeachment of President Clinton. Despite his moral condemnations of Clinton, it later became known that Hyde, although married, had had an affair. He dismissed it as a "youthful indiscretion." When the affair took place, Hyde was in his 40s.

Killing—The act of taking a life. The literal meaning would include all animal and even vegetable life. Anti-abortionists equate the termination of a pregnancy at any stage, even the earliest, with murder of a child or an adult. This is an extreme position, not widely accepted, but the language nonetheless does tend often to create an apologetic tone in defenses of abortion. However extreme, this usage has been somewhat successful as a propaganda tool for anti-abortionists.

Misogyny—Hatred of women; implied in many practices and laws, especially those forbidding abortion.

Modern Monetary Theory (MMT)—A theory recognizing that taxation is important (for example, for regulation, avoiding inflation, or regulating income inequality) but denying that it is important to finance government. Sovereign governments that create their own currency do create it as they spend. Receiving huge tax revenues does not enhance the government's ability to spend, nor does "deficit" spending

ABORTION AND INFORMED COMMON SENSE

reduce it. As prominent economist Stephanie Kelton puts it, anything that is technically feasible is financially affordable.

Modern Political Economy—Operating the economy for maximum benefit for all. Plan programs to be the most effective, and function for the best benefit of society, not to be the most "cost effective." Also, plan, wherever possible, to make programs universal; ie, to benefit all, rather than targeted groups.

Pain, Fetal perception of—Anti-Abortionists allege that a fetus feels pain. Science does not verify this, but there should be use of analgesic drugs during abortion to be certain that there is no causing of pain

Personhood—Not a scientific term. It has no biological meaning, and means merely whatever the observer's private opinion may be regarding what it is that constitutes a "person." Attempts to use scientific arguments to justify "personhood" at any stage of pregnancy are nonsensical.

Planned Parenthood—Organization founded by Margaret Sanger to provide women's health. It is the largest provider of women's health in the country. Abortion services are a minor portion of the health service it provides.

Planned Parenthood v. Casey (1992)—Upheld constitutionality of Roe v. Wade, but also permitted states to impose limitations, such as to require waiting periods, counselling, etc.

Roe v, Wade (1973)—Asserted unconstitutionality of anti-abortion laws based on a right to privacy; there can be no restrictions in the first trimester, some permitted in the second with woman's health taken into consideration, and full restrictions permitted in the third, but abortion may be permitted then if required for a woman's health and well-being.

Romney, Mitt—Senator from Utah, former Governor of Massa-
chusetts, Republican candidate for president in 2012 (the
only Mormon candidate), losing to Barack Obama. Son of
Michigan governor and prominent Republican auto CEO,
George Romney. Rare among Republicans, the conservative
Romney occasionally will stand up to Trump.

Rushdoony, Rousas John—Harsh, ultra right wing Calvinist
theologian, creator of Dominionism, or Christian Recon-
structionism, who argued for a stark theocracy with a huge
range of capital offenses and an aggressive foreign policy. Dominionist doctrines influenced other conservatives whose
extremism is not so overt, despite Francis Shaeffer thinking
he was clinically insane (according to Schaeffer son Frank).

Ryan, Paul—Former Republican speaker of the House, Republican candidate for vice president in 2012; reputation as a policy wonk; but shallow with little knowledge beyond talking
points. A Roman Catholic (despite devotion to the doctrines
of the militantly atheistic sexual predator Ayn Rand), he ran
on the Republican ticket with Mormon Mitt Romney.

Sanger, Margaret—Early 20th century advocate of women's rights
and birth control; founder of Planned Parenthood.

Schaeffer, Frank—An early arch conservative evangelist and maker
of religious films, son of Francis, who persuaded his father
to oppose, and then convince leading American Protestant
fundamentalist/evangelicals to oppose abortion, melding
Protestant extremists with Catholics united by anti-abortion activism; recanted when he recognized the dangerous
and totalitarian forces he encouraged, and regrets the harm
that he did; he remains a Christian (Greek Orthodox), but
campaigns strongly against the religious right and its harsh
policies, including anti-abortion policies.

Schaeffer, Francis—Charismatic evangelist, responsible for much of the political activity among Protestant fundamentalist/evangelicals, and for much of the anti-abortion obsession; father of Frank.

Texas Senate Bill 8—Harsh anti-abortion statute forbidding abortion after six weeks if a "fetal heartbeat" can be detected; unconventional, in that it empowers any citizen to enforce the law; it dies so by authorizing anyone to bring a lawsuit against any person providing or facilitating an abortion; if lawsuit is successful, the person sued would be liable for up to $10,000.

Thirteenth Amendment—Forbids slavery.

Tiller, George—Physician who provided abortions; murdered by anti-abortion fanatic.

INDEX

L

"L'Abri," 35

LaHaye, Tim, 38

Lakoff, George, 55

Language, 43-61

LaPierre, Wayne, 104

Liberty, pandemic restrictions seen as infringements of, x

Lincoln, Abraham, 56, 93-96

Lippman, Walter, 62

Loewen, James, 83-84

Logical contradiction, acceptance of, 69-70

Lynchings, 83-84

M

Manchin, Joe, 45, 101

Mattox, Pam, 91-92

Maryland, 8

Mask wearing, x

Mass movements, 75

Massacre by firearm, 48

Massengill Company, 30

McConnell, Mitch, 8, 14-15, 61, 100

Medicaid, 33-34

Medicare, 43-44

Medicare for all, 80-81

Medical clinics, bombing of 93

Mexico, 29

Midwest, 84

Military-Industrial Complex, 85

Misogyny, x, 22, 23, 40

Mississippi anti-abortion law, see *Dobbs*

Missouri, statehood for, 1

Model Mugging, 110

Monetary theory, 71

Mothers Against Malicious Acts (MAMA), 107

Mormons, 75

Murder, abortion equated with, 2, 92-93

N

National Advocates for Pregnant Women, 87

National Association of Manufacturers, 63

National Rifle Association, 7, 104-105

Native Americans, 82

Nazis, 24-25, 79

Needle-exchange programs, 72

New Deal, 34

New York Times, 16, 54

On self defense, 106-109

Constitution, suggestions for amendments, 1

Pure Food and Drug Act, 26

Q

Question of Choice, A, 29

Quickening, 21

R

Racism in America, 65

Reagan, Ronald, xv-xvi, 30, 37-38, 73

Reed, Ralph, 38

Regimentation, x

Reign of witches, 31

Republican Party, x, xv-xvi, xviii, 73, 90

    Court packing by, 8, 14

    Degradation of, 8, 10-11

    Extremism in, 3, 8, 76

    Need to oppose, 17-18

    NRA influenced, 104

    Obsession with Trump, 73-74

    Reality-based community, rejection of, 74

    Voter suppression, 60

Religion as politics, 38

    Dominant in most right-wing states, 73

Resentment against government, x

Richards-Merrell Pharmaceuticals, 25

Right-wing governments, 73

Rights, ix. xiv, 7

    Extra rights before birth, 1-2, 49-50, 86-87

    Women's, 1-2

Robertson, Pat, 37, 38

Roe v. *Wade,* 6, 7, 28-29, 33, 36, 82, 90, 96

Roman Catholic Church, see Catholic Church

Roosevelt, Franklin D., 44, 79-82

Rogers, Will, 21

Rushdooney, Rousas John, 35

Ryan, Paul, 71

S

"Safe Harbor laws," 15-16, 89

"Safety net," 43-44

Saloons, 84

Schaeffer, Frank, 35-41

    Success in politicizing evangelicals, 75

Schaeffer, Francis, 35-40

Science, misuse of, 13-14

Science denial, 13, 70, 71

Science, lacking in anti-abortion arguments, xiii-xiv

Schlesinger, Arthur, 58-59

Second Amendment, 104

"Second Amendment Remedy," 5

New Titles from Westphalia Press

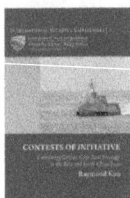

Contests of Initiative: Countering China's Gray Zone Strategy in the East and South China Seas
by Dr. Raymond Kuo

China is engaged in a widespread assertion of sovereignty in the South and East China Seas. It employs a "gray zone" strategy: using coercive but sub-conventional military power to drive off challengers and prevent escalation, while simultaneously seizing territory and asserting maritime control.

Frontline Diplomacy: A Memoir of a Foreign Service Officer in the Middle East
by William A. Rugh

In short vignettes, this book describes how American diplomats working in the Middle East dealt with a variety of challenges over the last decades of the 20th century. Each of the vignettes concludes with an insight about diplomatic practice derived from the experience.

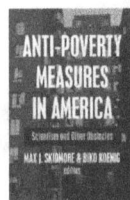

Anti-Poverty Measures in America: Scientism and Other Obstacles
Editors, Max J. Skidmore and Biko Koenig

Anti-Poverty Measures in America brings together a remarkable collection of essays dealing with the inhibiting effects of scientism, an over-dependence on scientific methodology that is prevalent in the social sciences, and other obstacles to anti-poverty legislation.

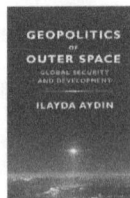

Geopolitics of Outer Space: Global Security and Development
by Ilayda Aydin

A desire for increased security and rapid development is driving nation-states to engage in an intensifying competition for the unique assets of space. This book analyses the Chinese-American space discourse from the lenses of international relations theory, history and political psychology to explore these questions.

Bunker Diplomacy: An Arab-American in the U.S. Foreign Service
by Nabeel Khoury

After twenty-five years in the Foreign Service, Dr. Nabeel A. Khoury retired from the U.S. Department of State in 2013 with the rank of Minister Counselor. In his last overseas posting, Khoury served as deputy chief of mission at the U.S. embassy in Yemen (2004-2007).

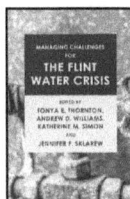

Managing Challenges for the Flint Water Crisis
Edited by Toyna E. Thornton, Andrew D. Williams, Katherine M. Simon, Jennifer F. Sklarew

This edited volume examines several public management and intergovernmental failures, with particular attention on social, political, and financial impacts. Understanding disaster meaning, even causality, is essential to the problem-solving process.

Growing Inequality: Bridging Complex Systems, Population Health, and Health Disparities
Editors: George A. Kaplan, Ana V. Diez Roux, Carl P. Simon, and Sandro Galea

Why is America's health is poorer than the health of other wealthy countries and why health inequities persist despite our efforts? In this book, researchers report on groundbreaking insights to simulate how these determinants come together to produce levels of population health and disparities and test new solutions.

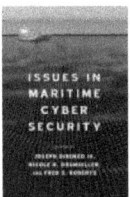

Issues in Maritime Cyber Security
Edited by Dr. Joe DiRenzo III, Dr. Nicole K. Drumhiller, and Dr. Fred S. Roberts

The complexity of making MTS safe from cyber attack is daunting and the need for all stakeholders in both government (at all levels) and private industry to be involved in cyber security is more significant than ever as the use of the MTS continues to grow.

The Politics of Impeachment
Margaret Tseng, Editor

This volume addresses the increased political nature of impeachment. Offering a wide overview of impeachment on the federal and state level, it includes: the politics of bringing impeachment articles forward, the politicized impeachment proceedings, the political nature of how one conducts oneself during the proceedings and the political fallout afterwards.

www.ingramcontent.com/pod-product-compliance
Lightning Source LLC
Chambersburg PA
CBHW060459280326
41933CB00014B/2796